Jack,

This is Johns second book. Great short stories we can both relate to.

Merry Christmas 2016

Your friend

Norman

WE'LL DO IT TOMORROW
Southern Hunting and Fishing Stories

By

John P. Faris, Jr.

Cover Painting
and
Illustrations
By
Nancy Kochenower

First published by Dog Ear Publishing
4011 Vincennes Road
Indianapolis, Indiana 46268
www.dogearpublishing.net

ISBN: 978-1-4575-4866-6

This book is printed on acid-free paper.

Printed in the United States of America

This is an Our Home Place, Inc. book.

www.outdoorstories.com

Also by John P. Faris, Jr.

Ten Was The Deal
Dog Ear Publishing
Indianapolis, Indiana 2013.

John P. Faris, Jr. also contributed a story
to *Outdoor Adventures in the Upcountry*, Hub City Press,
Spartanburg, South Carolina 2010.

... choose you this day whom ye will serve; ...but as for me and my house, we will serve the Lord.

Joshua 24:15
King James Version

Contents

DEDICATED

to

WILLIAM WEST WOODSON
September 7, 1983 – September 7, 1991

William taught me to never take tomorrow for granted. Time is a gift from God. Only He can give it. I invite you to read "We'll Do It Tomorrow" on page 25.

I shall pass through this world but once. Any good therefore that I can do or any kindness that I can show to any human being, let me do it now. Let me neither defer nor neglect it, for I shall not pass this way again.

Stephen Grellet

FOREWORD BY BOB TIMBERLAKE

When I first read *Ten Was The Deal*, I felt a very special kinship to John Faris. We've known each other for some years now, have shared some of the same great outdoor experiences, and now this second book "We'll Do It Tomorrow" really again jogs my memory of how I felt when I first saw my favorite movie – "Stand By Me" and read for the first of many times, Robert Ruark's *The Old Man and The Boy*. I had the feeling that the movie, Ruark's book, and now these two books, were written about me, my growing up on those who "grew" me up for these last eighty years. (I'm still working on the growing up part.)

While I'm nine years older and three hours north of him, it seems John and I grew up together and traveled most of the same wonderful paths. I, too, had my South Carolina driver's license at fourteen and was fishing, hunting, exploring, camping, trapping, and carousing all over North Carolina, South Carolina, and North America. I'm still at it, trying to grow up and catch up on whatever I might have missed before now.

In 1952 at Hampton Plantation in "lower" South Carolina, I sat at South Carolina Poet Laureate Archibald Rutledge's feet when I was fifteen years old and listened to his Low Country stories and his version of "The Secrets of the Forests." Now, I have from John, these same feelings and delights brought back after sixty-five years.

Mr. Shakespeare said it best: "I can no answer make, but thanks, and thanks, and ever thanks," to John for this new book and the brought back smells of bream beds on a hot summer late afternoon on a still farm pond. Our world.

Bob Timberlake

The Lord is happiest when His children are at play.
                    As told to Bob by Charles Kuralt while fishing.

INTRODUCTION

When I wrote my first book, *Ten Was The Deal*, in 2013, I was surprised at its success. I received not only nice book reviews and complimentary comments from folks that you would expect to gravitate to hunting and fishing stories, but many non-hunters, women and men, spoke of how much they enjoyed word pictures of our beautiful southern outdoors, of the closeness and companionship of those we spend days afield with, and the adventure that is so much a part of many of our hunting and fishing trips.

This book is more than tales of turkeys, rabbits, deer, ducks, and fish. It is about the joys and sorrows of life itself.

I hope you will enjoy these stories as much as the experiences I had living them and reliving them as I share them with you, the reader.

AMONG A THOUSAND

The Reedy River passed under State Road S-30-36 not far from Ware Shoals at a place known as Ekom Beach. When the weather was warm and the days long, folks from all over Laurens County came to this unusually wide place in the river. They enjoyed summer supper and swam in the cool, smooth flowing water just off the sandbar created by the sharp bend in the river – hence the name Ekom Beach.

That was during the summer.

When winter came, the Reedy ran hard, deep, and cold. It became chalky-gray. When the rains came in late November and December and the water got up, this river could be a killer. The current rushed even faster then, cutting the steep banks away and causing old-growth trees to cave into the river, their limbs catching all manner of brush and debris. Surging through these obstacles, the water sped up, foamed, and grew loud. It sucked everything that floated within its reach down into the depths and held it there in its powerful hydraulics and backwashes.

The Reedy was both playground and grave.

Early in the duck season Sammy, my hunting partner who was one year younger, and I did not hunt the Reedy regularly. First, it was a good four-mile walk from the let-out bridge to Burton Pond, the next place you could get to the road. Secondly, there was no thought of wading the Reedy for a downed duck. On smaller rivers and creeks, one of us would strip off our boots, socks, underwear, and pants, and wade the icy water, naked from the waist down, to retrieve our prize. Not the Reedy. No one would be that crazy. In the '50s, good shells were a nickel a piece. You picked your shots carefully. If you didn't shoot the ducks so they drifted near the bank, it was just a lost duck – not something taken lightly. The clincher, though, was that many times after temperatures dropped, the Reedy could often be slap full of acorn-fat mallards and blacks. As the season wore on, the temptation was just too irresistible. We hunted the big water.

The stretch from the Highway 30-36 bridge to Burton Pond was a wild stretch of twisting river, steep hills, big swamps, and vast canebreaks.

As the river pushed its way toward Lake Greenwood, it cut sharply away from all roads on the stretch from Ekom Beach to Burton Pond. From either side of the river it was a very long walk from any access road. Therefore this section of the Reedy lay in one of the most sparsely settled parts of our county. No people lived on this section where we hunted except maybe, just maybe, one family.

When we hunted the Reedy we were traveling what old folks claimed was an Indian trading route. Even older trails, they claimed, were made by the buffalo as they followed the river from one canebreak to the next. Vast numbers of buffalo had cut sections along the riverside trail. It was so worn down that when Sammy and I walked through these narrow paths, we would be almost waist-deep below the surrounding ground level.

It was quite an adventure to make this hunt with my boyhood partner, Sammy. Prior to our becoming driving age, Sammy's granddaddy, Mr. Boyd, would put us out at the bridge.

The two of us would make the four-hour hunt to Burton Pond. Sammy's granddaddy would then drive further downriver, park off the tar-and-gravel road, and walk the short quarter-mile down the sloping ridge to Burton Pond. There Mr. Boyd would wait for passing shots of ducks we might flush in his direction. We made this hunt often toward the end of the season and normally collected our limit. The ducks were so plentiful and the hunt so much of an adventure that the Reedy drew us back again and again.

One of the most dangerous aspects of these trips was created by two unusual geological features. First, about half-way between the let-out and pickup point was a natural swamp off the right side of the river. This swamp was created by the river cutting across, at its narrowest point, a large loop in its winding course. Once cut off from the flowing water, the loop had silted in, creating an oxbow. The second feature was a steep, sheer rocky cliff that formed the lower end of the swamp.

The inlet to this swamp, right where the water from the old oxbow met and emptied into the river, was very narrow, only about eight feet wide. Two of the largest poplar trees I have ever seen served as bookends for the channel. I have always believed these twins may have been the tallest trees in our county. They were not only tall, but they were also big, big beyond description, in circumference. The two giants were joined by a narrow hand-hewn timber that appeared to be quite ancient. Joining these two trees about three feet above normal water level, the beam served as a footbridge. This spot was the only path downriver without going a long way around the swamp. The unanswered mystery was the identity of the person who had conceived this footbridge and when it had been placed here.

From the looks of it, many years earlier someone had cleverly fashioned a crude but substantial wooden frame supported by the big timber on the top and the two poplar trees on either side. The sturdy wooden gate mounted to it could be raised or lowered. Closed, the gate held back all the water in that flooded twelve-acre swamp. If it was raised, the water of the Reedy could flow in when the river came up high or the water in the swamp could flow out as the river went down.

The gate allowed its operator to manipulate the water level, forming either a very large lake in the swamp or a marshland that never went completely dry.

It was not hard to imagine the gate being raised during a heavy rain and the swamp flooding as the river rose. Fish would follow the rising water and food into the swamp. We could also picture a net being placed over the frame, the river level dropping, and the gate being opened. All the fish that had followed the water in would be trapped in the net as they tried to escape the falling water. Ducks would be just as susceptible to this water level manipulation device. When left as a marsh, seed-producing grasses would spring forth and flourish until flooded in the late fall. A waterfowl mecca would result.

It was easy to see that large numbers of fresh fish and waterfowl had been lured into the swamp over the decades. Sammy and I speculated that many an early Native American family had lived off the bounty.

This spot was truly interesting. Game-rich, old, mysterious, and a little scary. Part of the mystery was the keeper of the gate. Sammy's granddad, who had hunted this same stretch of river for five decades, said an Indian family was believed to live on top of the steep bluff overlooking the swamp. He speculated it was they who hunted, trapped, and fished this watershed. Sammy and I had seen the gate to the fish trap both in its raised and its lowered position, so we suspected at least part of that family still lived near the swamp.

Our path down the river led us over the narrow timber of the fish trap. We had to balance ourselves and tightrope across, ever mindful that on our left was the fast-running main river and, on the right, the deep swamp channel.

Falling off the footbridge in cold weather was not an option. Two people together offered some semblance of safety. First, we could hold our partner's outstretched hand partway across giving us some comfort; and second, if you fell in, at least there was someone who could try to save your life. Weighted down with several layers of cold weather clothes, hip boots, pockets full of twelve-gauge shells and a gun, I was always grateful for a buddy as I walked across that narrow footbridge above the frigid water.

Once across the fish trap timber, an even scarier section lay ahead – the cliff trail. Just as we stepped off the timber footbridge, the old Indian trading route angled up the rocky outcrop. Over the many years countless human feet had worn a narrow toehold across its face. The trail ascended sharply until it was well over forty feet above the Reedy. The highest point on the trail was still another two hundred feet to the top of the small mountain. The river, over thousands of years, had literally sliced this mountain in two as it made a sharp left-hand turn. Where the river swung against the rock face that made up this granite wall, it was hard to imagine how deep the water would be at the base and how fast the current was accelerating.

No significant vegetation – no trees or shrubs – grew below the narrow rocky ledge though a few old tree roots were visible. That is to say, almost nothing would break a fall. It was a fearful, intimidating place.

I always hated this part of the trip down the Reedy, and I suspected Sammy did also. However, at twelve and thirteen years old, we would never have admitted this to a soul, let alone to one another. As scary as this section was, we gave little thought to climbing straight up the cliff and cutting over the mountain. It would have taken us an extra forty minutes and a lot of effort even if we had known what lay in that direction. We had been warned on numerous occasions not to go messing around the top of that mountain.

A certain mystique remained about what was on the mountain or who, if anyone, actually lived there. Sammy's granddaddy was the only person we knew who had ever been over the mountain, and that had been at least four decades earlier. He told us an old Indian man, along with his son and daughter, lived on top of the steep bluff over-looking the swamp. His story was sketchy at best.

Supposedly, before Lake Greenwood was built, an Indian family had lived on a small fertile farm along the original game-rich Reedy River valley. Their farm was in a very isolated part of the county; and the family, pretty much self-sufficient, stayed to themselves. When the valley was flooded in the early '30s, more people began visiting the new lake. Building lots were sold, and money was made off the land. Small fishing shacks and modest summer cabins began to appear along the shoreline.

Supposedly a dispute arose over the rightful ownership of the land this Indian family had lived on for years. Because they couldn't produce a deed of any kind, the Greenwood sheriff finally ordered the family of four – two teenage children and their Cherokee parents – off their farm. The family was forced to move five miles to the even more remote and undesirable piece of land high above the Reedy River. That was in the '30s. The father and mother had died years later, but the young daughter and her slightly older brother had stayed on the land.

In and of itself this story would not have left the lingering feeling of mystery about the people of the mountain, but three decades after the Indian farm had begun to be sold off, one after another mysterious fires occurred. No structure on the farm, no matter how small, was ever completely finished before it went up in flames.

In 1959 when Sammy and I were hunting that old farmstead on Greenwood Lake, not a single structure remained on that stretch of the lakeshore even though the rest of the lake was beginning to develop. The subject would often come up about buying a piece of that beautiful undeveloped shoreline, but someone would eventually say, "You don't want to fool with that crazy Indian. Buy somewhere else."

Sammy's granddaddy said he didn't know how much of this story was actually true because a thriving moonshine business was also running out of this section of the county. Moonshiners are not known to embrace close neighbors either. Those of us who hunted there had a very healthy respect for anyone who might call this land home.

As for Sammy and me, we stayed off the mountain.

Once past the swamp and cliff, we knew the best part of the entire hunt lay ahead. All the way to Burton Pond the river spread out, got wider, and calmed down some. Tree falls occurred less often, and endless pin oak trees grew with their duck- drawing, bite-sized brown-and-gold acorns.

Sammy and I would often say to each other, "If you had enough acorns you could pull a group of mallards up a concrete road."

It was this stretch of river that enticed us to brave the narrow footbridge and the slippery, narrow crossing at what we named Indian Mountain.

As Sammy and I grew a little older and I got my driving permit, my family bought a six-cylinder black Nova station wagon that sorta' became my car. Sammy and I quickly gravitated to the freedom of driving ourselves when and where we wanted to hunt. Little was safe on the water or in the woods after that – fish, ducks, rabbit, quail, or squirrels. It really didn't matter. Whatever was in season, we were after it. One slight drawback to this new-found freedom, however, was that Sammy or I would now have to take turns getting out at the bridge and walking the stretch down the Reedy alone.

For some reason on the first trip of this new arrangement, I was the one to start at Ekom Beach. Even though he was not supposed to, Sammy drove the car to Burton Pond. When I set out at the bridge that day I knew it would be a good day. It was cool, clear, and the river not too high. I could already see handfuls of water oak acorns on the limbs that were eye-level to the old high bridge. The morning sun knocked off the chill as I walked, and the light hunting coat I wore would offer just enough protection to keep me warm.

By the time I reached Indian Mountain, I had spotted two mallards ahead on the river. Their V-shaped wakes on the sunlit surface in a long straightaway section gave them away.

Though they were seventy-five yards ahead, I was very careful and slow as I slipped down the river. They did not detect my presence. The banks of the river were steep where the pair was feeding, so I eased out away from the river, cut inland, and headed straight back to the river where I thought they would be. Luck was with me when, hidden by the high bank, I popped out right on top of them. They flushed and three feet off the water both fell at the bark of my Browning 12-gauge. I laid my gun down and slid through the thin bushes on the bank holding on to a protruding poplar root, stretched way out, and retrieved both mallards as they drifted by me.

I stuffed both acorn-fattened drakes in the back of my hunting coat, taking satisfaction in the new weight I felt. They accounted for numbers twenty-six and twenty-seven of my season total. I heard Sammy shoot three times way down river. When I finally started over the footbridge timber, I didn't think too long about crossing it. Holding my gun in my right hand and stretching out my left hand like a tightrope walker, I scooted across without looking down. As I started toward the cliff path, however, I got cold feet. That fifty-yard path and deadly forty-foot drop into quarreling icy cold water convinced me to back up. I only thought about it a brief moment and headed instead up the mountain. I did not care what was up there, or the time it would take to reach Sammy by going in this direction. I was not going over that usual path by myself.

To get up the treacherous terrain I actually had to reverse my direction and begin the slow climb on the other side of the swamp. Thirty minutes later and a little out of breath, I came out on a surprisingly large, relatively flat meadow. From where I stood it spread out about ten acres before the land turned sharply up the mountain again.

I needed to go left to get back on my downriver path; but as I headed in that direction, I suddenly noticed, tucked just inside the timberline, a small log cabin and several outbuildings. My path along the meadow would, by necessity, take me very close to this little homestead. As I approached I was very cautious, watching, but mostly listening, for farmhouse dogs. People raised in the country from a very early age, know to be wary of entering a person's homesite without letting the owner call in or quiet their dogs. Driving up to a house in the country and jumping quickly out of the car could send a visitor straight to the hospital.

People own a farmyard dog for a purpose. Protecting their turf is priority number one. I knew if the cabin was occupied and if the inhabitants owned a dog, the canine sentry would hear me long before I would see it. I waited a full five minutes at the edge of the meadow just listening.

No barking erupted so I eased along the edge of the meadow. The wind shifted slightly, offering my first whiff of wood smoke – just a trace. But I now knew I was not alone. As I got closer, the details came into focus – a cabin made of broad, hand-hewed logs, a split-shingled roof, a trail of smoke from the rock chimney, and a big garden to the right. The sunlight revealed dried corn and okra stalks, wooden stakes supporting long-dead tomato plants, and a row of fresh mustard greens. Bright purple tops of a few turnips stuck out of the dark, soft earth. A split-rail trellis was covered in dried gourd vines.

Once I was even with the homestead, I noticed an herb garden near the right side of the cabin. It had been planted in a large wooden wagon wheel of years ago. The wheel had been filled with loamy soil, and each spoke separated a different fresh herb from its neighbor. I did not know them all but could recognize mint, thyme, chives, and rosemary.

I passed close to an open shed containing a wooden work surface that was still wet where someone had rinsed it off not long before. Dried gourds were stacked in one corner, and long pine needles were soaking in a bucket of water. This work area backed up to a low, log outbuilding displaying a number of steel leg traps hanging from wooden pegs.

Several raccoon skins and one mink skin were drying on stretcher boards, and more gourds were drying on a wooden shelf. Several large bunches of white onions, their tops braided together, had been hung on wooden pegs to dry as well.

I looked around once more, pretty sure I was being watched. Surprisingly, I did not feel frightened.

For some reason I will never know, I reached into the pocket of my hunting coat, took out three shotgun shells, and stood them in a line on the still damp table. The 12-gauge high brass magnum fours we called Blue Peters. I looked toward the cabin once more before moving through the hardwood timber and easing back down to the river.

I collected a summer duck a mile further down before Sammy and I rendezvoused at Burton Pond. We had three ducks each.

I never told Sammy about my fear of the mountain ledge, my trip over the mountain, or the cabin and its outbuildings. My excuse for taking longer was that his longer legs allowed him to walk faster. This part was actually true.

Two weekends later it was my time again to start at the bridge. I reached the footbridge timber and noticed the open fish gate. The river did not look so dangerous with the water low and clear. I scooted across the narrow timber without even a thought to the ledge, then turned and hoofed it up over the mountain and out on the meadow's edge before stopping to catch my breath and listen. Five minutes passed. Nothing, no sound save the light breeze whispering through leafless hardwoods.

I felt more comfortable about trespassing on this tranquil scene than before, but only slightly. When I came alongside the work table, I stopped dead in my tracks. There on the table were three empty blue hulls of the shells I had left two weeks before to the day. They had each been shot, picked up, and brought back here.

The more shocking thing, however, was that they were arranged in a perfect line. In the center was a handcarved wooden feather painted as if a real bluejay had just dropped it. Even to my young, untrained eye, I knew the feather was a work of art that had taken a long time to make. I instinctively knew it had been left for me.

I looked carefully around. I had not fired one shot while traveling along the river to the fish trap.

How did anyone know I was coming? I asked myself.

I took three new shells out of my canvas hunting coat, replaced the empty hulls with the unspent bullets, and carefully placed the feather in my left shirt pocket. I arranged the new shells in the same pattern I had found the empties and headed down the mountain.

Action picked up on the lower Reedy. I heard Sammy cut loose, shooting four times which told me he must be into more than a small group of ducks. I quickly chose an opening right on the bank of the river with no tree branches above so as to get a clean shot if the ducks Sammy had flushed were escaping upriver toward my position.

Sure enough, a half minute later six mallards flew by, circled once, and actually lit on the water not fifty yards above where I stood. Well camouflaged, I stood very still.

After waiting several minutes to confirm if they were now safe, all six – four beautifully iridescent green heads with bright indigo chevrons on their wings and two neatly camouflaged hens with persimmon beaks – began floating in the current right to me.

Afraid to wait too long as they would actually get too close, I shot one bull drake at twenty yards on the water and got two more, one about even with the bank's top and the last one among the water oak branches. As I scooped the last of the ducks out of

the frigid water, I tucked the head and neck of each under one of its wings and neatly placed them into my coat's rear game pocket.

Sammy was waiting for me, leaning against a riverside snag. His game pocket was bulging, but mine was pretty heavy too. I could tell he was trying to judge the damage to the waterfowl population I had inflicted by staring at my coat, as I was his.

"All right, out with it. How many?" he asked.

"Let's head up the hill and wait on the night flight. I'll tell you all about it on the way," I replied.

Turns out Sammy had gotten quite close to a large group of unsuspecting mallards resting on a sandbar in a sharp curve above Burton Pond. He had slipped in and killed two with his first shot and gotten two more as they flushed upriver.

Standing in the crisp December twilight, we watched the evening star, accompanied by a honey-colored moon, rise above the Reedy River bottoms. I told Sammy my story of the hunt as a purple and crimson sunset silhouetted droves of ducks aiming for the big water to roost. We couldn't wait to come back.

When it snowed the following Wednesday, school was cancelled. With the roads closed, Mom forbade driving. Thursday was better and after much persuading, she acquiesced to my begging to let Sammy and me go hunting. I reasoned that we were having terrific luck on the Reedy that season and that we had never hunted there before in the snow. Sammy's mom, however, refused, saying it was too rough driving and he had some unfinished chores. I failed to say anything to Mom about Sammy's absence. I had decided to hunt the Reedy alone.

When I reached the high bridge I parked the Nova station wagon on the opposite side of the road a couple hundred yards down from the bridge. No use advertising to the world that ducks galore were just below the crossing.

It is hard to describe what five inches of fresh snow does to a river bottom. It muffles almost all sound. It is so quiet in the woods you can hear your own breathing. You move with silent steps through the stillness as if you are the shadow of a ghost. All things look different too. The river, now chalky-gray, flows between broad, white shoulders. All sharp edges are gone, rounded and softened by a thick layer of white. Familiar landmarks become altered, and the riverside trail disappears. It is an eerie, but intoxicatingly beautiful scene. It is a lonely place, but you don't feel lonesome. This new world seems to be frozen in time, but those that make this area home must find food amidst this wonderland. Caution is cast aside by every living creature about the serious business of staying alive. The ducks are no exception.

Almost before I lost sight of the bridge, I began flushing up groups of duck. I had never seen so many, and I could be picky with my shots. Only the big bull green-headed mallards were my target. I was one short of my limit by the time I reached the fish trap. Since I was hunting alone and would have to retrace my steps back to the bridge, I subconsciously calculated the time it would take to get back to the car. My decision was to hunt a little further past the trap.

It was a bad decision.

I started across the timber. With the blanket of snow, the footbridge looked wider than it was. The soft snow also disguised the slick solid ice beneath. Two steps out on the familiar crossing, my left foot began to slide toward the deep, cold river water. My reflexes were good. I quickly reacted but overcorrected and fell toward the swamp side, my right leg sliding between the bridge timber and the fish gate.

Before I could even process what was happening, I found myself pretty much upside down, hanging by my right leg only inches from the iced-over water of the swamp.

First thought - *Nothing's broken. My leg hurts a lot, but not broken.*

Second thought, *I am not in the freezing water – yet.*

Third thought, *It's only nine o'clock in the morning, and I'm alone.*

I was somewhat thankful that it wasn't close to dark and the colder weather sure to come. I was also somewhat unnerved that no one was expecting me for hours and hours.

With all the adrenaline rushing in my system, I convinced myself I could get out of this mess. But my left leg was useless, my right leg was caught, and I could do nothing to pull up or push off of with my arms and hands. Then I became vaguely aware that with my head lower than the rest of my body, I was becoming lightheaded and disoriented. I was losing focus.

Then darkness! Excited voices, bad pain, then more darkness. Lying in the snow – cold – like making snow angels, then I blacked out again. Slowly I returned from the darkness, warmer now, to the smell of wood smoke.

A soft soothing voice, "You're okay now. We brought you to our cabin to get warm. You've been unconscious about an hour. How's your leg?"

The voice belonged to a slender woman about my mom's age. Looking over her shoulder was a slightly older man, wearing a red and black flannel shirt, faded jeans, and knee-high rubber boots. Firelight from the hearth accentuated their ruddy complexions. Though I did not know these people, I knew I owed them my life. Pushing up off the blanket-covered bed onto one elbow, I winced at the pain and had to lower my head between my knees for a minute.

As my head cleared, I asked, "How'd you find me?"

Before they could answer I added, "Thank you for helping me. I'm John."

The man answered, "I'm Luke. My sister is named Sarah. Our parents were Christians and named us from the Bible. While checking my traps this morning, I saw you along the river. You and your friend hunt the river often. You're both good hunters. You're the boy who leaves shotgun shells at the skinning table. I was working the inside edge of the swamp as you hunted the other side and was not far behind you when you reached the footbridge. I saw you fall but couldn't get you up by myself. It took me twenty minutes to get Sarah. It's lucky your leg hung in the gate, or you'd have fallen through the ice into the deep channel of the swamp. You wouldn't have lasted long."

Sarah came from the stove with an enamel cup. The steam rising from it smelled of apple and cinnamon.

Luke asked, "Can you stand on your right leg?"

When offered, I took his calloused hand and pulled. As I put weight on my leg, it hurt pretty good, but I could walk. No permanent damage. While I struggled to get my boot back on my right foot, Luke brought over my gun which had, by some miracle, gotten hung in the gate when I fell. He had also oiled it after cleaning off the snow. The six mallards that had fallen out of my hunting coat had been retrieved, cleaned, and now lay in a blue-speckled enamel pan by the kitchen sink.

Sarah said, "I'll wrap up the ducks, and Luke can drive you back to the bridge. That leg's going to hurt for a while. Lucky it's not broken."

"Thank you both. I really thank you. Please, you keep the ducks. I don't know how I can repay you."

Sarah answered, "We're just glad we found you and that you are alright."

As I picked up my gun and hobbled toward the door, I noticed a thick wooden shelf of the gourd bowls – each one unique. They were beautifully made and carved with intricate designs colored with dye. Around the top rim, long, fresh pine needles had been bunched and wrapped with a single pine needle forming a smooth round brown rope. These were attached to the top of the bowl forming a finished round lip, all sewn to the bowl with more pine needles. Each was a magnificent work of art.

I turned to Sarah and asked, "The bowls are beautiful. Who makes them?"

"Luke and I make them together in the winter months from the gourds we grow. Luke cuts the tops out, cleans them, and drills the holes in the rim. I sand them and paint the designs. Our mother taught us how to do this."

"They are truly beautiful."

I followed Luke to the shed where a 1951 black Ford pickup was parked. Together we headed across the untouched snow-covered meadow with Luke expertly nursing the truck in low gear up through the deep woods. Traveling on the winding forest road it was slow going. I asked Luke where this road came out because I had never known of another way to the river.

He paused and smiled slightly, "I'll show you but please keep it to yourself. My sister and I came here when we were quite young and don't want any trouble. We've been on the land for close to forty years but have no papers. It's building up fast down on the lake now, and we may have trouble someday."

As we approached the highway, the dirt road ran right into the back of an old wooden barn. The other end of the barn came out not fifty yards from a gate that bordered State Road S-30-36. Luke drove through the gate, looked carefully both ways, and turned right. I looked back over my shoulder at the barn and caught Luke in a smile. I had driven past that barn dozens of times and had never imagined a road might be behind it. Ten minutes later we were at my car.

Before I opened the door, I shook Luke's hand and said, "Luke, thank you and your sister. I'll never forget what you did. You probably saved my life. I promise I will not tell a soul about today or the road. Not ever. After today, I'm not sure I'll hunt this river again. I don't know."

I reached in the backseat of my car for the two new boxes of Blue Peters and handed them through the truck window to Luke. "Thanks again," I said.

Luke reached behind him and handed me a paper grocery sack. "Sarah and I want you to have this." I peeked inside and smiled. It was one of the handcrafted bowls.

"Luke, I can't take this gift. It's beautiful, but I have no way of explaining it to my parents. If they find out about my close call today, I'll never get to hunt in these woods again. Besides, I need to keep you and Sarah a secret too. Thank you so much though."

We both smiled. Luke waited to see that my car would start. As I eased it onto the snow-covered road, snow began falling again – the perfect excuse for me to be home early.

I never hunted the Reedy again. I created some humdinger excuses for Sammy, but I never hunted there again.

Two years later I drove down the Ekom Beach road to go fishing on Greenwood Lake. I passed over the high bridge and, looking down the river, remembered my last hunt there. I smiled as I thought of Luke and Sarah. As I reached the old barn site, however, I almost ran off the road. The barn was gone. A red clay road leading into the woods spoke of disaster. A big sign at the entrance read: COMING SOON – INDIAN MOUNTAIN CAMPGROUND PARK.

It had been dry for two weeks and the freshly cut road was still rough but drivable. I could not help myself. I backed up and eased down the road toward the meadow. I could not take it all in. The cabin and outbuildings were all destroyed – nothing but scorched bones. Everything was gone. Only the garden fence with the dried gourd vines remained.

I just knew they were both gone. Luke and Sarah would have left their home without any trouble, but they had burned it all down – leaving nothing behind.

For years I wondered where they might have gone. I also wondered if anyone else had ever found the fish trap and thought it an object of great interest. I wondered if anyone else had taken up hunting the Reedy from the high bridge to Burton Pond.

Five decades passed.

On a vacation to Santa Fe, New Mexico, with my wife, we strolled from shop to shop looking at some of the most beautiful Native American art I had ever seen. After looking at the prices, I shoved my hands deep in my pockets and kept them there lest I knock something over and break it.

The last shop we went in that morning was just to the right of the Loretto Chapel. It apparently specialized in antique Native American baskets and bowls. On a black pedestal prominently displayed under the glare of three track lights was a single masterpiece. I asked the shop owner where the bowl came from. She said many years ago a woman and her brother, Cherokee Indians from back east, had moved to town and sold the bowls made from gourds. The brother had died a few years back, but the sister still lived on the edge of town. Though quite elderly now, she still brought a bowl or two in ever so often to sell.

I returned to the pedestal and admired the workmanship. The bowl looked for all the world like the one from Indian Mountain that I had returned to Luke. I would have known it among a thousand.

WE'LL DO IT TOMORROW

The peaches, pinks, and purples of the sunset were mirrored in the wet sand of receding waves. It would be light enough this August evening on Pawleys Island, this three-mile slice of heaven along the South Carolina coast.

I was following the small footprints of my two young children, Ashley and John, and my seven-year-old nephew, William, in the warm seaside sand. William was the youngest of the three. He was my baby sister's first child. He was a handsome young boy with thick brown hair and beautiful bright brown eyes. He was a four-foot bundle of energy, full of curiosity and a thousand questions. Because my sister lived in Atlanta, I did not get to be with William much except at the beach on shared family vacations. He loved to be outdoors and anything I was doing from checking crab traps, throwing a cast net, to fishing in the surf, William was always by my side. He would say, "Let me do it, Uncle Johnny, let me do it."

The three cousins dashed ankle-deep into the dying edge of each wave, giggling and laughing at some made-up game they were playing. I was only half watching with my eyes. My mind was on tomorrow. I had been in charge of these three forever energized, mischievous rascals since early morning. Happy marriages offer trade-offs between busy moms and dads, and today was pay forward for the promise of a tomorrow all by myself surf fishing.

As the children danced twenty yards ahead, we worked our way toward the northern inlet of this barrier island. I was carrying my eleven-foot surf rod with a hammered finish, chrome Able spoon, clipped in the base of the first ferrule. When we reached the inlet, I planned to let the children play along in the fading light as I waded fifty yards or so further out on the spit of sand that separated the Atlantic Ocean from Pawleys Creek.

The day-trippers were long gone. Formations of brown pelicans were heading for North Island to roost, and the waves were pushing the falling tide into emerald haystacks.

I gave the standard parental instruction, "Y'all stay close, John, Ashley. Play right here for a few minutes while I go out and make a few casts. Don't get into trouble, and we'll make milk shakes when we get home. William, stay with John and Ashley, Okay?"

I began wading out. When I got knee-deep I freed the Able and turned the left-hand handle of the big Penn spinning reel. The right length for the one-ounce lure to load the rod was a foot from the reel tip. I flipped the bail and cast the silver missile sixty yards into the seaside surf.

I was not really fishing – if there is such a thing – only scouting for tomorrow.

After two more casts to the seaside with no encouragement, I tried in the creek's direction thinking that since the tide had turned and the rip was forming in that direction, it might just be the ticket to hook a hungry bluefish.

As I began to make my first retrieve I felt a sharp tug on the hem of my faded rolled up khaki pants. Having seen sharks cross this shallow spit on previous trips, I instinctively jumped and turned and looked down into the face of William who was wet to the bone.

"William, what are you doing way out here?"

No sooner had I finished my sentence than a crossing wave knocked him a little off balance.

"You are soaking wet. Your mother is going to kill me," I shouted above the crashing of the surf.

I continued retrieving the lure and saw him watching the revolving shiny spool. He pointed to it and begged, "Let me do it. Uncle Johnny, let me try."

"No, no." I told him. "The rod is much too big for a little guy." I glanced back to the beach to be sure that my two were still out of the water. An upset sister is one thing. An angry wife is quite another. Seeing they were still somewhat in place on the shore, I said "William hold on to my pants pocket. I'll just make a couple of casts, and we'll head back to the house."

I put the Able out into the middle of the increasingly more defined rip. Nothing.

"Please let me do it?" William begged, his eyes locked onto the big whirling spool.

"No. Let Uncle Johnny make just one more cast and we'll go. Are you cold?"

The last attempt produced nothing more than disappointment. As I held William's hand we slowly pushed our way through the falling chop over the bar. The water was late-summer warm, but the breeze made anything wet feel like forty degrees.

I gathered up my two children, still somewhat dry, and retraced our quarter-mile walk back to Snail's Pace, our summer house. Lights in oceanfront cottages winked on in increasing numbers as dusk faded into darkness.

My two children raced ahead, milk shake promises pulling them home. Still holding William's hand I could feel him trembling with the cold. I had nothing for him but "It won't be long 'til we'll be there."

Several times he begged "Me do it? Me do it, Uncle Johnny."

My final "No, William, we'll do it tomorrow!" had a little too much bite. His hand slipped from mine, and I wished the words back.

Just to break the silence I said, "William your mother is going to skin both of us alive. Just look at us! You are soaked!"

As we climbed the last of the steep steps over the dunes I said, "Go get some dry things on, and I'll get the milk shakes ready. You want vanilla or chocolate?"

"Vanilla," was the expected answer. His grandfather, my dad, loved vanilla ice cream, and William copied everything his beloved Dee Dee did.

As I slipped into the kitchen and fired up the forty-year-old Hamilton Beach blender, I could hear my sister all the way from the other end of the small house say "William, where in the world have you been? You are soaked! Come get in a hot shower right now!"

I was glad to be in another part of the house, away from her. I knew she would calm down a little while doing the shower thing.

I made three milk shakes, two chocolate and one vanilla. To soothe my conscience, the vanilla was extra large. I was determined to take William out in front of the house tomorrow, make a few casts, and let him reel the line in. I would make it all right.

Morning dawned with promise. Payback time. My day off. I fished the south end hard, then moved to the north end for a couple more hours with no better luck. By noon a dark front moved on a west wind. I made it to the house as the sand began to blow down the beach in lateral lines that stung my knees.

I was showering off some of the salt and sand under the house in the outside shower when my wife, Claudia, peeked over the wooden shower door and said, "Everyone thinks the rain has set in, and since this is the last day, we all think we should pack up and leave early."

It was an idea hard to argue against. The weather was growing worse with every passing minute. I packed the Oldsmobile station wagon in pouring rain. It made no difference. In ninety-five degree heat by the time I would have completed the loading of suitcases, beach toys, and fishing gear, I would have been soaking wet, no matter.

The next time the thought of William crossed my mind was late that night back at home in Spartanburg when I unpacked, washed, and cleaned the rod and reel. We would probably go back to Pawleys Labor Day for a final trip. I would make teaching William a priority then.

That trip never happened.

Instead a call came from my dad. Mom and Dad were immediately heading to Grady Memorial Hospital in downtown Atlanta. A car had hit William as he and his dad were leaving a Braves baseball game. William had massive head injuries and many broken bones. A nine-day vigil at the hospital by the family and friends followed.

I realized the extent of his injuries when on the second day the nurses asked my sister for a picture of William. They wanted to see what he looked like. I never went into the room where William lay. I did not have the courage.

On day ten William went to be with the Lord.

A week after the funeral my neighbor, a doctor, assured me that William's death was a blessing. My head told me so, but my heart would not accept it. A few days later, I sat beside my sister in her living room. She stared into nothingness. In a drugged monotone she mumbled, "We wanted to donate William's organs to maybe help some other child. When I asked the doctor what they were able to use, he looked at me and nervously said, 'Why Harriett, William was a healthy seven-year-old. There was nothing we could not use, eyes, skin, all the organs. We were able to use it all.'"

Harriett said she had turned to the doctor and said, "Eight."

The doctor said, "I'm sorry, I don't understand."

Harriett said "William was eight, not seven. He died on his birthday."

After two weeks of on-and-off private weeping, I did not think I could cry any more, but I was wrong.

Since that day I have been blessed to fish in many places around the world. I have caught and released some big fish. I have surf fished up and down the east coast many, many times. I have also returned to our seaside cottage on Pawleys Island several times a year for over twenty-four years, but I never pick up my surf rod and wade into the waves that I don't remind myself of my promise to William.

Until this day I have never told this story to my sister and the pledge I made to never, ever again, say to a child, "No, no. We'll do it tomorrow."

A BEAUTIFUL SHOT

In the late hours of Christmas Eve 1953, I could not sleep. Anticipation was running high. I was eight years old, but I had no inkling that on Christmas morning I was in for the best surprise of my young life. I would not discover until years later that my dad had spent several pre-Christmas months convincing my mom to let Santa Claus bring me a real gun, a .410 shotgun, to be exact.

Since I was six years old, I had been the proud owner of two Daisy BB air rifles, both gifts from Santa Claus – one Christmas apart. The first one was a little lever-action Red Ryder model with a wooden stock, wooden forearm, and open sights. In the 1950s it seemed every boy I knew got one of these BB guns for Christmas.

No matter what age a boy got his BB gun, it was the centerpiece of that year's visit from Santa. In Christmas night dreams, the little treasure would be propped up by the chimney or under the decorated cedar Christmas tree. Beside it would be a cardboard tube of fifty bright, shiny copper BBs inside the stocking along with perhaps an orange, apple, and small handful of hard candy. What more in this world could a boy want or expect? He had it all with Santa's gift!

My first Daisy was a wonderful gift to own. Most of the basic rules of gun safety and hunting I learned within the first twelve months with that lever-action air gun. Dad used it to instruct me. I learned about cocking it only when I was ready to shoot, about laying the gun flat on the ground before crawling under a fence, and never climbing over the fence with a gun in my hand. He taught me to never point the gun at anybody, and he demanded that I always have the barrel pointed in a safe direction. Dad showed me patience in taking a shot, and he made sure my face was down on the stock. He spent a lot of time teaching me about properly leading a moving target. We would practice this a lot behind our house. Dad would toss pinecones in a fast-moving stream. As they sped by I would try hitting the pinecones with my Daisy.

I took to owning a gun like a duck takes to water. As soon as I got the hang of the principle of leading a target, it was just a matter of practicing. Before long I was pretty good at it. In fact, I got so good that when next Christmas rolled around my newly acquired skills almost got my cousins and me into big trouble.

Once I understood how to lead a target with my BB gun, it was a short step to applying the idea to other moving targets. I had two sisters and four first cousins. We all lived on Main Street within a couple of blocks of each other so it wasn't unusual for us to be together, especially after school and on weekends.

When Christmas holiday came my dad arrived home one evening with a big bundle of fireworks including a large pack of rockets. These were no wimpy little bottle rockets. No, these rockets were a good eight inches long. They were about one-and-a-half inches in diameter, and they had a four-foot red wooden stick incorporated into the body of the rocket. They were designed to be launched from a five-foot section of one-inch pipe that had been driven into the ground. Normal operating procedure was to insert the red shaft into the upright pipe that pointed skyward, light the fast-burning fuse, and run for cover. For a brief second the rocket would sit in the pipe, spewing copious sparks and thick gray smoke. Then it would blast from the pipe, and shoot almost out of sight, straight up, exploding into a huge sphere of fire balls.

Well, when good dark came that night and all the cousins were present and accounted for, we began firing off the rockets. This wonderful display of power and speed held our attention for about ten minutes. It was then I decided to display my proficiency in leading a target.

My family lived on the corner of West Main Street and Barksdale Circle. Main Street ran in front of our house and a good number of cars passed by on a regular basis. Barksdale Circle was a smaller street that ran along our side yard. It came to a dead end at Main Street. Even though small, Barksdale Circle was a paved street with formed concrete curbs.

With a degree of superiority I demonstrated to my younger sisters and cousins that by laying one of the rockets flat down in the middle of Barksdale Circle and lighting the fuse, it would travel down Barksdale Circle at amazing speed instead of shooting straight up. If it veered off course, it would hit the curb on either the left or right side, correct its course, and shoot all the way across Main Street, hit the curb on the opposite side of Main, and explode into a spectacular fireball.

My sisters and cousins, who had lined up along Barksdale Circle as I fired off the first couple, were very impressed. They all almost passed out from laughing and giggling.

Not one to let the high drama of the moment be lost, I told Gregory, the older of my sisters, to go up to the end of Barksdale

right at Main Street and call out when the next car heading down
Main Street passed the big curve coming toward town.

Well, it only took me two cars to get the lead perfected. The
first rocket was about twenty yards behind the approaching car.
This only resulted in more hysterical laughter. The rocket I lit
next crossed about ten yards in front of its target, causing the driver to slam on brakes and swerve in a crazy manner. This sent all
of us running into the bushes to hide, laughing so hard we almost
wet our pants.

I had the lead figured out now.

On the third attempt the rocket ran true. My timing was
impeccable. The normal explosion was slightly muffled as it took
place directly under the unsuspecting Chevrolet sedan approximately midway between the front bumper and the driver's seat.
However, the shower of sparks was most dramatic as the bottom
of the car disrupted the normal explosion pattern. Instead the
result was a spectacular ring of alternating red and green fireballs
shooting out in every direction from under the hood. The seven
of us observed this pyrotechnic display just long enough to realize that if caught enjoying this dramatic climax, we would all
catch heck.

We ran like the wind to Aunt Laura's house, hid the balance
of the rockets, and as casually as possible slipped in the kitchen
door. Following some quick coaching, I sent my youngest sister
Harriett, to the den to ask Aunt Laura if she would make us some
hot chocolate. The homemade ginger cookies and cocoa gave the
seven of us good cover for the next hour.

When my Mom called for us three to come home, there was
a fire truck, a police cruiser, and a wrecker still at the intersection
of Main and Barksdale. They were routing traffic around the

wrecker from Wesley's Gulf Station as they worked to get the sedan on the hook.

As we went in the house, my two sisters cut their wide eyes over at me. I put my finger over my lips and said, "Shhhhhhhhh."

I didn't get much sleep that night. Ever so often one of us would think of that car that resembled a Roman candle going off. We would get tickled, and have to cover our heads with our pillows to keep from waking up Mom or Dad. This would set off a chain reaction till all three of us were in hysterics.

I guess Santa Claus thought I was learning pretty fast because the next Christmas I got a pump-style Daisy BB gun. This model had more power, a longer barrel, a peep sight and, in my opinion, a bit more accuracy. For the record, sixty-two years later, I still have both BB guns. They both work perfectly.

In the '50s our home was the last house on West Main Street and just within the city limits of Laurens, South Carolina. It stood on a large, wooded lot. No more houses had been built behind our backyard, so in this vacant land of grown-over field and woods, I learned to hunt. Mom was very strict about my not harming cardinals, thrushes, Carolina wrens, and mockingbirds. Everything else was fair game.

At six I was pretty big for my age, but I had a hard time cocking my Daisy at first. I had to put the butt of the stock on the ground against the outside of my left foot, hold the barrel straight up, and pull the lever with my right hand. It took all my power. After about three months though, I grew stronger and I could throw the stock behind my left thigh and cock that gun as fast as lightning.

I carried my treasure back into those woods every day after school. I learned to sit still, and let the woods settle down. Once done, the birds and animals would not pay me much notice. I learned a great deal about how critters behaved and reacted by just sitting very still and watching.

In those few surrounding acres, I could not have been happier had I been on an African safari.

About 6:30 A.M. false dawn finally came that Christmas morning in 1953. Mom and Dad had mandated that 6:30 A.M. was the absolute earliest that any of us children could get out of bed to see what Santa Claus had brought. In addition, part of the Christmas morning rules stated that I had to wake up my two younger sisters so we three could enter our den together. There Santa would have already come down the chimney, eaten the cookies we left on the hearth for him, and arranged the precious gifts.

It's funny what details a person recollects about important moments in life. The memory I have of that morning is of the most beautiful shotgun in the world leaning against the brick chimney. My eyes spotted a little .410 over/under. It had a single .410 barrel on the bottom and a single shot .22 caliber rifle barrel on top. It had open sights and a hammer that you cocked. Dad was not a big fan of rifles and I don't remember him buying me a single .22 rifle bullet.

Dad never let me cock the gun or take off the safety until I was ready to take a shot. He instilled that lesson in me from the very beginning, and I never broke his cardinal rule.

In the days following Christmas, I did a lot of weekend practicing of gun handling and shotgun shooting. Dad started me out on stationary targets. Then I graduated to hitting cans that he would throw up in the air for me.

Three weeks or so into January, Dad took me with him to a friend's house where he bought two old beagle rabbit dogs – Lady and Li'l Bit. I'm talking old and slow – long past their prime.

Though Lady could not see out of her left eye, and Li'l Bit was very hard of hearing, I did not care at all. As far as I was concerned, these two beagles were field trial champions.

We brought those two old veterans home. We ran them in the woods around the house on Sunday afternoons and sometimes when Dad got home from work during the week. On occasion the two dogs would chase a rabbit right through our backyard. Although enough woods and land surrounded our house for me to shoot the BB gun, we were still too close in town to use the .410. Even so, I was learning to work with the dogs and find rabbits.

About a month later, I guess my dad thought it was time for our first trial run with my new gun, the two old dogs, and, hopefully, a young rabbit.

Come one brisk Saturday afternoon, Dad loaded the dogs into a wooden crate in the trunk of the family car. We owned only one car and had no thought in the '50s of a pickup truck or what we now call an SUV. I carefully placed the .410 on the backseat and proceeded to get into the front passenger seat when out of the house came Mom.

Dad closed the trunk, came around to where I was sitting, and said, "Slide over and let your mom in."

I was very shocked. Mom had never been on any of our hunting trips before, not ever.

I thought, *Boy, this is something! Mom's going rabbit hunting!*

Later I came to learn that a condition of my getting the shotgun for Christmas was that Mom would at least go on the first outing and see how safe or dangerous hunting with my own gun was going to be. My mom's family was not big on hunting, so my getting a shotgun at eight was a big leap of faith for her.

My granddaddy on my mother's side owned a farm about ten miles out of Laurens on Yarborough Mill Road. A feller by the name of Shannon Eubanks lived on the land and sort of looked after things for Granddaddy, particularly the white-faced Hereford cows Granddaddy loved.

Well, when we got to the farm, Dad eased up the dirt road in front of Shannon's two-story, wooden clapboard house and honked the horn. More than a dozen raggedy-looking chickens of all colors, six or so black-and-white guinea hens, and several rawboned, long-eared hound dogs shot out from under the wraparound front porch, which served, it seemed, a good number of varied purposes.

A single bed with a very thin mattress, an old couch that I remember from my grandmother's sunroom, and a washing machine were on the porch. I was fascinated with the washing machine. Shannon's wife would use both hands to crank a wet pair of pants or a shirt through the two large wooden rollers.

Seeing those guinea hens scurrying out from under the house reminded me of a week earlier when Dad and I had been out on the Princeton Road. Running late coming home, Dad's foot was a little heavy on the gas when he topped a rise on the tar-and-gravel road right in front of Mr. Marcus Boyd's house. I figured we were going at least sixty about the time we topped the hill. A sizeable flock of guineas jumped off the red clay bank on the right. Our car and the biggest part of the flock collided. I turned around quickly in my seat to a view of dead guineas, their feathers flying in all directions. Dad took one quick look in the rearview mirror and floored the Plymouth. We never slowed up 'til we got to the main highway. Dried blood and a good many feathers remained stuck on the chrome grill of the car until after we got home. You can bet that little episode did not come up as a topic for table talk that night at supper.

Shannon appeared in his faded coveralls and worn denim jacket as the sagging screen door slammed shut. He slid in the backseat smelling of tobacco juice and sweat after a hard day's work outdoors. Dad eased his way through the panic-stricken chickens so as not to run over Shannon's supper, and we headed down to beautiful wide bottoms that lay along Warrior Creek.

Dad negotiated the Plymouth down a steep red clay road and pulled through a gap in the barbed wire fence. Shannon had moved the white-faced Hereford cows that my granddad loved so much to a new pasture that morning. Cautiously avoiding a minefield of fresh cow patties at the gap, Dad wisely drove out into the pasture a little before letting my mom exit the car.

As soon as we stopped, we all piled out, careful of where we placed our feet. When Dad opened the trunk I thought those two old beagles were going to tear the crate apart. Seems they had played this scene before, and the excitement put pep in their step that I had not yet witnessed.

Shannon lifted a big, long oak stick he carried most of the time. Without a word he led the dogs toward the swamp along the side of Warrior Creek and began to beat the bushes. His actions encouraged the dogs to get in there with him and find a big blue-footed swamp rabbit.

Meantime Dad nodded permission for me to slip a 3-inch No. 6 .410 shell in my gun. I closed the gun shut with a solid click and checked to be sure that the hammer was on safe.

I was being extra careful and deliberate because I felt Dad and I were both on trial that day. I was trying to remember everything I had been taught, be very careful, and impress my mom.

Well, it wasn't long before old Lady struck a rabbit out in the swamp. Li'l Bit joined in hot pursuit on that rabbit's trail, carrying him to ride. Shannon's yelling and hollering the dogs along seemed to just put more fire under the kettle. Before I was old enough to carry a gun I had gone with my dad and his hunting buddies many times. I have always been thrilled when hearing our dogs push a rabbit along. The sound of the two old dogs was music to my ears. The howls of Lady and Li'l Bit now left no doubt they were on a hot trail. They sounded nearly frantic. I glanced at Mom and knew she was really getting into the excitement, too.

I had already learned from running the dogs in our backyard that if left to the rabbit's own devices, he would make a wide loop, then head back toward the place where he was first jumped.

Mom, Dad, and I were about twenty yards out in the pasture from the swamp's edge. A rusty, hog wire fence ran along the swamp to keep the cows out of the creek. When the dogs jumped the rabbit it had sense enough to run toward the swamp and through the holes in the hog wire. The dogs were too big to go through the fence. That old rabbit thought he had it made until Shannon picked each dog up, fairly flinging them over the fence. The race was back on! The rabbit, with the dogs pushing him hard, finally made his circle and headed back toward the pasture. My anticipation was ratcheting up by the second as the pitch of Shannon's hollering and the barking of the dogs increased and came closer and closer.

Dad encouraged me to step a little nearer to the hog wire fence running along the swamp, get out in front of Mom and him, but stay about fifteen yards back from the wood line. I quickly followed his advice, got in position, and placed my thumb on the gun's hammer.

It won't be long now, I thought.

Sure enough about that time that old swamp rabbit shot between the holes in that hog wire fence, spotted me, turned a hard left, and shot down that fence line like his tail was on fire. He was moving so fast it looked like he was not even touching the ground – just flying. I cocked the hammer and cut down on him going flat out. When that load of No. 6 shot caught up with him, he cut a flip head over heels and rolled a good ten yards.

I was so proud of myself. This was my first experience as a real hunter, and my dad's training had really paid off. The shot I had just made impressed Mom and probably even Dad.

I dashed over, picked up the rabbit, and held it high for all to see. Lady and Li'l Bit joined Dad, Mom and me in the excitement.

Dad patted me on the back, and I heard the pride in his voice, "Good job, Sonny Bo. Good job. That was great!"

With a smile I'll never forget, Mom, put her arms around me, dead rabbit and all, gave me a big hug and said, "Your father has taught you well. I think you're ready. That was a beautiful shot!"

OUR SECRET

The shot came from just ahead. A powerful hand pushed my face into the damp, cold dirt, and a voice insisted, "Stay down! Stay down!" It was the morning of November 26, 1955.

My dad had a group of close friends – contemporaries of his – that hunted rabbits almost every Saturday during the season. Every weekend from Thanksgiving to the first of March, I joined them. At nine years old I was the second youngest member.

On this particular fall Saturday a very traditional football game was played at Sirrine Stadium in Greenville, South Carolina, between the Clemson Tigers and the Furman Purple Hurricanes. My mom's side of the family was very much interested in team sports. Basketball, baseball, and football. College football was high on their list. My mother's Dad always bought tickets for my mom, my dad, and he and my grandmother to go to this Furman home game, which started at two o'clock in the afternoon. I did not care a thing about that football game. I was dying to go rabbit hunting with our group. Even though my dad was a graduate of Furman, he was lukewarm on the idea. After talking to my mom, he realized he would have heck to pay if he did not escort her in this annual tradition.

It was decided. Dad would drive everyone to the game, and the family would have a grand day at Furman. As a point

of negotiation, however, my dad convinced my mom that the two of us would get up even earlier that morning and go with our usual crowd rabbit hunting. The trade-off was a firm promise that we would return home in plenty of time for Dad to get cleaned up and dressed for the big game. In those days proper dress for a college football game required the men to wear coats and ties. Women wore stylish wool suits, high heels, and usually a corsage displaying the colors of their favorite team. In this case, my grandfather had bought two – in Furman's royal purple and white – one for my grandmother and one for my mother.

So that was the plan. Dad and I awoke with much anticipation on Saturday morning. We met Dad's friends at the home of Carlos Boyd who lived on Chestnut Street in Laurens, South Carolina. Going there was just about the most fun a nine-year-old boy could have. Their land had a creek running through it where Bud, Carlos' son and my friend, would set traps for possums and coons.

The Boyds always had multiple projects in progress, like the building of duck boxes and rabbit gums. I was fascinated by critters like their pet crow, usually a litter of pups, and a wild bobcat that frightened me just to look at it. We knew how the duck season was shaping up because Bud nailed the head of every duck any of the six of us killed on the outside wall of their board and batten workshop.

No matter the season, there was a large manicured vegetable garden in the rich bottomland dirt next to the creek. No one could escape the Boyds' hospitality. Everyone visiting received a generous mess of turnip greens or collards in the fall, tomatoes and Blue Lake string beans in the summer.

Mr. Boyd and Bud kept the rabbit dogs – fifteen or so long-legged beagles – at their house. The rest of the group helped with the dog food and vet bills. These dogs were probably one of the best packs I ever hunted with during my childhood and youth. We did a lot of rabbit hunting so I knew a good pack of rabbit dogs when I saw and, more importantly, heard them.

That morning we helped load up the dogs in Carlos' green Chevrolet pickup and headed down to Cross Hill. Mink Brown – one of our regular group – was in the lumber business. He bought a lot of timber from a Mr. Hollingsworth down in Cross Hill and, therefore, we had access to prime rabbit hunting country. We arrived to perfect rabbit hunting weather – cold and cloudy. It had rained the night before so the fields would be a little bit wet. The rabbits would leave a strong scent on the cool, damp ground. The dogs would be able to follow the trail very well and the cold temperature would keep the pack from getting overheated. We knew we were in for some great hunting.

We were in the field by 8:00 A.M. with the dogs immediately jumping a rabbit not twenty-yards from the truck. I can remember two of the grown-ups in our group killing a couple of rabbits pretty quickly. Since we weren't too far away from the truck yet, it was senseless to carry those fat rabbits all day long. The men asked me to take their kill back to the truck and hang them on a nearby tree limb.

Not wanting to miss a minute of the hunt, when I got to the truck I hurriedly prepared those rabbits. I took my pocket knife and made a small slit right below one knee joint on each of the rabbits' legs. I cut two small green limbs off of a nearby tree, threaded them through the leg slits, and hung the rabbits up in the cold fresh air. They would hang there until we returned to head home.

It didn't take me long to catch back up with the hunting party. I could tell exactly where they were because the men would often encourage the dogs to hunt in the thick places with loud hoots and hollers that the dogs recognized. Our good rabbit dogs would enter a briar patch, take the thicket apart, and pretty soon jump a rabbit. So by the time I reached the group they had topped a little hill and started into some thin woods along the sixty-acre broom straw field they had just crossed.

I began walking right beside my dad – very close to his side. The dogs jumped another rabbit. The hunter closest to the dogs called in the entire pack by hollering at the top of his voice, "Here ya-go, here ya-go, here ya-go."

All the dogs had been well trained on that call and immediately rallied behind the jump dog. Within a second or two, all fifteen excited dogs joined in the race.

Clearly from the sound of the pack, the rabbit was coming directly towards Dad and me. No doubt it would pass very close to us.

I was shaking because I knew I would definitely get a shot. As I began cocking my gun, I heard a shot. Instantly my dad pushed me to the ground, forcing my face into the cold, wet dirt. I was so anxious to shoot the rabbit. I could tell it was coming right towards me. Why was Dad pushing my face down, down into the dirt?

Dad hollered loudly, "Don't shoot, don't shoot!"

To me he kept insisting, "Stay down! Stay down!"

I can still remember how cold and damp the ground was at that moment. I kept trying to get up because I wanted to see the rabbit come by. I wanted to take a shot. Within seconds the dogs passed not fifteen yards from where I lay. Knowing the rabbit had already passed, Dad finally let me get up.

"Dad, why'd you keep me down? I could have killed that rabbit!" I complained. Turning to face him, I then saw that he was bleeding from his left cheek – bleeding pretty good, I might add. Dad kept touching his cheek and smearing blood everywhere on his face as he felt the wound.

With shock and fear I asked, "Dad, what happened to you? Why are you bleeding?"

"I've been shot," he mumbled.

His answer really stunned me. The men in our hunting group were very experienced and had always been careful hunters. I never dreamed any of us would ever get shot. It had never crossed my mind.

The group quickly surrounded Dad, asking question after question about what had happened.

Not wanting anyone to make a big fuss, Dad stated in a matter-of-fact way, "I've been shot. I'll be okay but I got to take the boy home."

It was obvious Dad had not been mortally wounded, but the side of his face was really bleeding. Everybody offered to take us back to town, but Dad refused, "No, I'll be okay," he repeated. "I just need to get the boy home."

We hurriedly walked the good half mile back to Dad's Plymouth and drove home at top speed. All the way there Dad kept dabbing at his cheek and poking his tongue in the pellet hole. It looked as if he had a big plug of tobacco in that cheek. When he began to bleed out of his mouth, I became even more frightened. I had never seen anybody get shot before, much less my dad.

Heck, when somebody gets shot, that's a big deal!

When we reached Laurens, instead of driving straight to our house, Dad turned at the next street over, into the back parking lot of Dr. Reeves' office on West Main Street, just to the right of our house on the adjacent corner. The office was not open on Saturday, but it so happened the doctor's car was there. When

Dad knocked on the back door, Dr. Reeves took one look at Dad's face and pulled us inside, asking Dad "What in the world happened?" Dad told him about being shot.

Dr. Reeves led us back to the first examining room and cleaned Dad's face with some cotton soaked in alcohol.

"Well, I don't think it looks too bad, but I need to look inside your mouth." He pulled Dad's cheek out with one of those wooden tongue depressors, and said, "Hmm, I see where the shot went in your gum and lodged under one of your teeth." Dr. Reeves said, "I think I can get it out, but I need to give you a shot of Novocain first. It's going to hurt."

Pulling his jacket sleeve up and looking at his Timex watch, Dad said, "No, no, we don't have time to do that. I gotta go to a football game in a little bit." Dad said, "I've got less than an hour to get ready to go. We need to make this quick!"

Unsure he had heard my dad correctly, Dr. Reeves questioned, "You sure you want me to try this without the Novocain? It's going to really hurt, and you'll have to be very still."

Dad replied, "Yeah, let's get going. It'll be fine."

Dad was always tough when it came to dealing with pain. He had been severely injured in the Second World War – suffering a broken neck. He had lived with real pain for years. On several occasions while growing up, I had seen him black out from the pain in his head. I never remember seeing him take anything more than half an aspirin, and only then in very rare circumstances.

Dr. Reeves assumed I was up to serving as his assistant. He handed me a little stainless steel pan containing some instruments and instructed me to just sit on the stool next to my dad. Wearing one of those head mirrors on his forehead so he could see well, he grabbed a sharp knife from that pan and started to cut

Dad's gum open. I realized that he was going to reach where the bullet had gone in and pull the pellet out.

I remember thinking, *This is not going to be good!* I was getting a little light-headed, but I was determined to do my job as nurse.

Dr. Reeves next selected a pair of tweezers out of the pan and reached into my dad's mouth. All the while I could hear my dad breathing hard through his nose. I could tell the doctor was hurting him a lot, but Dad was being really brave about it.

Only seconds later Dr. Reeves sighed, "I got it." He held it up in the bright white light and dropped the pellet into the steel pan. I fainted on the spot, fell off the stool, and hit my head hard on the tile floor. Now the doctor had two patients to look after.

I guess I wasn't out but just a little bit. Next thing I remember, I was back on the stool with a cold rag wrapped around my face.

Dad didn't even let the doctor put a Band-Aid on his cheek. Dr. Reeves rubbed some sort of chalky looking stuff on the outside of Dad's cheek that caused it to stop all the bleeding. You could not tell from the outside that anything had happened to my Dad. I had a pretty good bump coming up on the back of my head, but my hunting cap covered that.

Dad and I slipped out the doctor's back door and got in our car. But instead of going straight to our house, he drove around the block and he instructed me very carefully that we could not tell anybody, EVER, about his getting shot or about my fainting. If anyone found out what happened, we would probably never get to go hunting again. I completely understood the need for keeping quiet. My mom and her non-hunting side of the family were not too keen about my being in the woods with my own shotgun at such an early age anyway. I knew Dad was absolutely right about never mentioning our little adventure.

Dad and I both tried to walk into the house as nonchalantly as we could. I avoided answering any questions about our early morning hunt by going straight to my room and cleaning both our guns, my normal responsibility. Dad made a quick trip straight to the bathroom where he took a hurried shower.

Both of my parents dressed to the hilt for the day. Dad wore his favorite sports jacket, tie, vest, and gray felt hat. Mom looked pretty spiffy too. She had been, I think, getting ready since we left that morning. As Dad opened the front door for Mom, he caught my eye, smiled, winced just a little, then winked. My dad and I had successfully buried the truth and thereby lived to hunt another day!

Dad and I hunted together until he was ninety-three years old. I turned seventy this hunting season. This is the first time I have ever told our secret.

Bigger Fish To Fry

This story originally appeared in
Ten Was The Deal
It is included here for the readers who
may not yet have been introduced to Savannah.
Illustrations by Ralph Mark

Shimmering silvery moonlight rode the ripples into ever-expanding circles. The fish slowly moved forward, the top of his tail and dorsal fin now sticking out of the skinny water. He was easing closer to his target.

Scarcely ten yards away, I was sitting in a small wooden boat, fly rod across my lap, watching the drama unfold.

I had been hitting the bream beds around the shallow edges of my grandfather's seven-acre lake since half past four. It was now nine o'clock at night. Using my fiberglass L.L. Bean mail-order fly rod and a small, orange, rubber spider, I had collected thirty or so double-hand-size shellcrackers. I was quietly paddling back up the far side of the lake when the water's movement first caught my eye. The deep croaking of a lovesick bullfrog echoed from the direction of the ripples. It was almost dark. A full moon sat balanced atop the old-growth trees on the hill above the boathouse.

Another series of croaks and I was able to pick out the big, deep-voiced frog sitting on a tiny, grassy island just off the bank. The water was no more than hand deep where he sat. Old Bully was really letting it roll, broadcasting to all the females where he was and that he was more than ready for their companionship.

It was early summer and courtship filled the air. He felt safe on his private island in that very shallow water.

He was wrong. Dead wrong.

As the frog was midway into a particularly loud and long series of croaks, the bass made his move. With strong thrusts of his tail he surged through the water and mud, rapidly crossing the six-foot distance to his supper.

Mr. Bullfrog saw the impending doom, but he had not sensed the danger in time. The fish made one more mighty push of his powerful tail, and was airborne. The frog sprang from his little kingdom as the half-gallon, Mason-jar-size mouth inhaled the frog's head and the front two-thirds of his shiny, slick green body. Only the long, now helpless, hind legs protruded from the bass's mouth as he fell on muddy, but solid ground. Legs still kicking from his mouth, the bass arched his powerful body back and forth, back and forth, as he flopped toward the water. Mud went flying everywhere. Finally the huge fish, with supper deep in his throat, reached the shallow water again and righted himself. Once more the mirrored surface of the lake was broken as the bass wiggled the last few feet back into deeper water.

As I sat there and watched the moonlight catch the final ripples, I took a deep breath. Two thoughts crossed my mind. First, I had seen the largest largemouth bass I would probably ever see in my life. Second, I would spend the rest of that summer trying to catch Mr. Record Breaker.

That was Saturday. Little did I know that Sunday was to be another memorable day.

Savannah had been in our small town for two weeks when I first met her in that summer of 1959. At eighteen, she was four years older than I was. I would learn that she was much different than the girls I had grown up with and who were in my high school classes.

Savannah had arrived from Italy where she was living with her father, a colonel in the United States Army serving with the Diplomatic Corps. Savannah had been in boarding school in Paris for three years and now was to spend the entire three months of summer with her aging grandfather, Mr. Ashburn. I wondered how Savannah would take to our small Southern town with the entire population being approximately 6,000, counting every man, woman, and child.

I was quite surprised to meet her. It was on a warm, summer Sunday morning. Mr. Ashburn, Savannah's paternal grandfather, lived in an older brick house across from the First Baptist Church on West Main Street where my mother's entire family, for several generations, had been members. The adults of my family were considered pillars of the church. In a small-town Southern Baptist church, this meant total involvement from the cradle to the grave. My family and I attended services at least three times every week. Members of the family taught Sunday School classes, cooked casseroles for Wednesday night suppers, and played the piano or led the singing at prayer meetings.

As children we were not allowed to play cards, go to the picture show, or hunt on Sundays. For some unfathomable reason, however, we were allowed to go fishing on Sunday, after church of course. I always wondered if it had something to do with the majority of the deacons of the church being big fishermen, but not regular hunters.

It was my custom on most Sunday mornings to leave right after my Sunday School class was over, run across the street to Mr. Ashburn's house, and talk about fishing, both Mr. Ashburn's and my favorite subject. These weekly visits lasted about twenty minutes. Then it was off to join my family in the morning worship service, which lasted until noon or longer if the preacher got really wound up.

Mr. Ashburn, who was confined to a wheelchair now, had been an avid freshwater fly fisherman through the years, and his fishing stories fascinated me. I loved those brief weekly meetings, but this warm, sunny, June Sunday morning my visit was to be different.

As I knocked on the door and started to let myself in, I almost ran over Savannah. I said, "Excuse me." And I took a step back toward the door.

Just then Mr. Ashburn called from the sitting room on the east side of the house, "Johnny is that you? Come on back."

The attractive young girl who stood in the doorway stepped aside slightly, and I walked past her, went through the darkened front room and into the bright, sunlit sitting room. It was Mr. Ashburn's favorite place.

As I entered the room, Mr. Ashburn said, "Oh! I see you've met my granddaughter already." As I looked over my shoulder I could see she had followed me into the room.

"Johnny, I want you to get to know Savannah. She is here for a while."

I awkwardly stuck out my right hand. She looked at my hand for a split second before taking it in hers. She gave me a very firm, no-nonsense handshake.

61

Mr. Ashburn continued, "I hope you will help me entertain Savannah this summer. I'm an old man, and she'll be bored to death hanging around here with me. Please do take her to meet some of your friends."

As her grandfather spoke, Savannah sat down on a low ottoman beside her grandfather. She was almost as tall as I was. Her long, straight hair touched the middle of her back. It was the color of polished ebony. Her skin had the look of a perpetual summer tan. There was an ever so slight oriental appearance to her high cheekbones and dark eyes. As she sat on the low foot-stool, she stretched her long legs out, crossed them at the ankles, and leaned back on her hands. The only thing about Savannah that remotely reminded me of any of the girls I went to Laurens High School with was her long-sleeved white blouse and faded blue jeans. She had yet to speak a word.

Mr. Ashburn and I were dyed-in-the-wool fly fishermen, an uncommon sport in the late '50s. It never became very popular in our part of South Carolina. Mr. Ashburn, my father, and I were perhaps the only three fishermen in town that I knew who used a fly rod. My dad began teaching me when I was eight years old. Six years later, with many hours on the water under my dad's tutelage, I was almost as good as he was. My dad was a very good fly fisherman.

By this time I was a true believer in fly-fishing. Delicately laying the proper fly down at the end of a long well-executed cast was the most deadly fishing technique I had ever tried.

Oh, don't misunderstand. I would quite often slip a five-inch night crawler, green and yellow Catawba worm, or a fat cricket on a long shank hook tied to a limber Calcutta cane pole and wear out a bream bed. I was certainly happy to cast a closed face Zebco reel loaded with a ten-inch-long Black Magic Pork

Rind to every hungry bass in the pond. I was not above hand cutting a piece of my mom's fatback into frog-shaped legs and slapping the still-smooth surface of after-dark bass haunts with a jigger pole. But given the option, fly-fishing was my passion.

Mr. Ashburn and I visited a few minutes, and it didn't take long for the conversation to turn to fishing. I told him of the great bream and bluegill fishing that was still going on, but had, as usual, peaked on the full moon in May. He wanted to know what flies they had hit best and what time of day the fish were feeding.

It was not the pan fish I wanted to talk about. Instead I excitedly told him of the extraordinary largemouth bass that I had seen chasing minnows up in the shallow grass late last evening. In explicit detail I shared the exciting episode of the frog.

As I told the story, I occasionally stole a glance at Savannah. She seemed surprisingly interested. As the time came to go to church, I rose and said to Mr. Ashburn that I would see him next week.

To my utter amazement, I heard myself say, "Savannah, would you like to go fishing this afternoon?"

The first words I heard her speak that summer were, "Yes, I would."

I looked at my Timex watch and said, "I'll pick you up at three o'clock. What you have on will be fine. Long sleeves and long pants will be best if it's buggy."

I turned and let myself out.

Church seemed to last forever. Mother's fried chicken with homemade milk gravy, rice, garden fresh green beans, and creamed corn were top on my list. But the meal seemed to take an eternity to get to the table this Sunday.

At last, by two o'clock, I was packing up my 5-weight fly rod, two cane poles, a small wooden tackle box that I had made in my Dad's downstairs woodworking shop, my favorite paddle, two seat cushions, the wire fish basket, and a small wire bait bucket.

Four months earlier I had gotten my permanent driver's license. I was allowed to drive the six-cylinder, black Nova station wagon, our family's backup car.

My mother was ecstatic that I now had aged up to my driver's license. I no longer had to beg her to drop me off and pick me up at remote farm ponds or lakes. Once I got my license at age fourteen, in Laurens County no fish or duck was safe. My driver's license and that little station wagon were gifts straight from heaven, of that I was sure. They were sorta payback for suffering through long, hot, summer Sunday morning worship services and weekly piano lessons.

I pulled up to 305 West Main Street at three o'clock sharp. Savannah was right on time. When I knocked on the door she appeared instantly. She was wearing the same outfit she had on that morning with the addition of short, well-worn hiking boots. She had rolled up her sleeves and tied her hair back in a long ponytail. As I had been taught by my dad, I opened the car door for her. By the time I got to my side, she had rolled down her window and pushed the vent window fully out to catch the breeze. With her arm propped on the open windowsill, she looked as if she were getting in this car and going with me for the hundredth time. I instantly felt as comfortable with this stranger as she seemed to be with me.

It was then, for the first of many times that brief summer, I noted I could tell when Savannah was near, even if I could not see her. It was like something in the air around her. She wore no perfume. There was no hint of soap or shampoo. Whatever the fragrance was, in the heat of the car that June afternoon it was totally intoxicating. Unlike the girls I had grown up knowing, with Savannah there was nothing to cause any expectation of our relationship, either short- or long-term.

It was simply a beautiful summer afternoon, and we were just going fishing!

As I started the car I asked her if she had been fishing before. She answered that her father had taught her many things, but fishing was not one of them.

"Don't worry" I said, "I'll show you how. We should catch some nice-size shellcrackers or bluegills. They're called bream around here, and they've been really hitting the crickets these last few weeks."

I turned the car around and headed out Greenwood Road to Bolt's Bait Shop. We would pass two other bait shops on the way, but Bolt's was the best place to buy fresh bait. It was built under a group of large poplar trees on a shady slope which dropped to a tumbling stream close to the back of the bait shop.

We pulled up, stopping well within the shade of the trees. I let the back window of the station wagon down, got the bait bucket out, and said, "Come on in. We'll get some crickets and something cold to drink."

The small building had that quiet, cluttered feel of all country stores. It offered just about anything you could imagine for a day on the lake. There were shelves of brightly hand-painted corks, display cards of black-and-white porcupine quill floats, and hooks in small die cut boxes either all the same size or in assortments. There were sinkers of all shapes and sizes from the smallest split shot on up. An array of various length shellacked cane poles hung in racks from the wooden rafters. There were small glass jars of dyed pork rind in black, green, and dark purple colors. There were cardboard displays of white and yellow Shyster spinning baits. Glass-front cabinets held boxes of individual plugs like Jitterbugs, Hawaiian Wigglers, River Runts, and Pal-O-Mine Minnows.

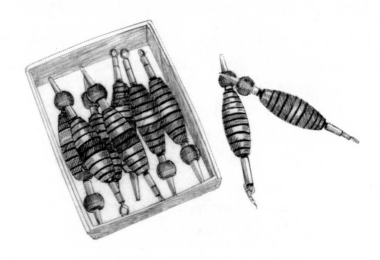

It was a place where a fisherman could spend hours.

Today, however, I only needed four dozen fresh live crickets, so I led Savannah through the small backdoor. An ad for Merita Bread was stenciled on the screen.

We stepped down into the coolness of the live bait area. Years before, Mr. Bolt had terraced the slope of the hill behind the shop down to the creek. He had hand poured concrete on each level to create a series of terraces and walkways with long, narrow concrete tanks for the minnows. Each size of minnow had its own tank. Cool water was pumped from the creek below and into the tanks through one-inch galvanized pipe with small holes. This caused the water to splash and bubble into each tank, giving the minnows extra oxygen. That made them very lively. They would be hard to catch if not for the small hand-dip nets that hung above each tank.

On the third and lowest terrace, just above the noisy little creek, was the wooden cricket cage. Inside the screen-wired cage was a small, bare lightbulb. Hundreds of chirping, jumping crickets were drawn to its warmth. There was no net here, just a small glass tube graduated on the side to show the number of dozen crickets the tube held. This tube had a large red funnel that fit into its top.

We waited for Mr. Bolt. He was very particular about his live bait. He was out front pumping gas. There was no self-service. A dollar's worth of gas in those days was enough to drive to Greenwood Lake, spend the day, and drive back with plenty of gas to get to work the coming week.

When Mr. Bolt finished with his customer, he met us at the cricket cage. "Johnny," he asked, "How many you want this afternoon?"

"Four dozen will be okay today," I replied.

There was a piece of gray cardboard egg carton at one end of the cricket cage near the light. Dozens of the crickets were attracted to the carton and would climb onto it. Mr. Bolt expertly picked up that carton and tapped it on the red funnel. A hoard of crickets fell and filled the glass tube. He then held it to the light, dumped out about two inches of the insects, held it up again, and thumped the glass tube with his forefinger. After sighting the four-dozen line, he tilted the tube over the cage, tapped on the tube until two crickets fell out, and sighted one more time. He thumped the tube again with his finger and caused the crickets to settle at the appropriate four-dozen level. You would have thought Mr. Bolt and I were trading in top quality diamonds. Finally he allowed me to hold my wire bait bucket while he dumped the crickets in.

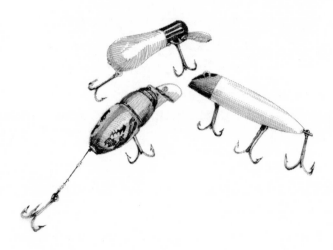

Savannah and I followed Mr. Bolt up to the cash register. I headed toward the Coca-Cola box, and asked Savannah if she wanted a Coke. She said no, but she would like a cold beer. As I turned to her I saw Mr. Bolt's head pop up and look at her from behind the cash register.

I lowered my voice whispering, "They don't sell beer here, Savannah. Besides, you can't buy beer until you're eighteen."

"I am eighteen," she said.

"Well, it's Sunday, and you can't buy beer on Sunday no matter how old you are," I explained. "They have Coca-Cola, Dr. Pepper, Orange Crush, 7-Up, and Cream Soda," I added, as we peered down at the brightly colored caps of the bottles almost submerged in a tub of ice-cold water. As she selected a six-ounce Coca-Cola, I pulled a twelve-ounce Dr. Pepper out, and picked up for each of us a Moon Pie on the way to the cash register.

When we got to the counter I said to Mr. Bolt, "This is Mr. Ashburn's granddaughter, Savannah, and she's staying with her grandfather for a while. She's from Italy." I quickly added, hopefully by way of explanation.

Mr. Bolt gave Savannah an up-and-down look, a little too long, I thought. He then glanced back at me and raised one eyebrow. I shifted my gaze and studied the basket of crickets as if I had never seen any before.

As Mr. Bolt gave me my change, I looked up at him. He glanced at Savannah once more. Raising that eyebrow again, he said, "Good luck."

My granddad's farm was on the Yarborough Mill Road. By the time we had finished off the sodas and Moon Pies, I was pulling the little black station wagon up to the white, wooden gate. The dirt road beyond led to the lake. I got out, unlocked the chained gate, drove through, stopped just inside, got out, and carefully closed the gate.

Granddad raised registered whiteface Hereford cows, and it wouldn't do for them to be scattered all over Yarborough Mill Road. That lesson had been hard learned last summer when I had not latched the gate properly.

I was with my dad that trip. He was driving. In the country it is proper etiquette for the youngest in the pickup truck or car to get out and open and close the gate. No young person, girl or boy, raised in the country, would ever think of sitting still as the vehicle approached a closed gate. They would immediately hop out to undo the gate and then close it back.

I remembered that particular day. After my dad drove through the gate, I closed it. In my haste I did not latch it back well enough. After Dad slowly eased the car through the herd of big cows congregated near the gate, they must have bumped it. While we were fishing that evening, the gate swung open. At nine o'clock that night Dad and I were still trying to round up thirty-four prize Herefords off the tar-and-gravel road and back into the pasture.

Dad and I agreed never to tell my grandfather.

It was a short downhill drive past the big barn, past the tall, hand-laid rock silo, through the virgin stand of red and white oaks to the ridge overlooking one of the most beautiful and productive man-made lakes I have ever known.

I was only a young boy when the lake was built, but I could recall much of the planning and construction. Before the dam was begun, a swift, bold stream wound its way through a long, heavily wooded narrow valley. My dad often took me out on Sunday afternoons to see the progress as the lake took shape.

First, all the trees had to be cut and burned. The two-foot-wide corrugated drain pipe was then laid in a bed of red clay right where the creek bed was. The dam was then built wide enough to drive a farm tractor across. For a small boy it was fascinating to watch the lake being constructed and to see the water slowly beginning to fill it. One month, two, three, then four, and still there was much area to be filled.

It was at about the fifth month when Granddad had the post and pilings set for the two boathouses and the fishing dock. It was also about this time, with the water still eight to ten feet from filling the lake, that my dad and I would walk along the rising water's edge. Dad let me guess where I thought the water would finally come as we looked at the remaining trees, newly-cut stumps, flat grassy meadows, and steep rocky ridges. We tried to envision and imprint in our minds for all time, what these last few feet of shore would look like once covered by water forever. Old intersecting gullies would be transformed into inviting coves, grassy meadows would become shallow fish-feeding flats, and steep ridges would become cool deep lunker hideouts in the late summer heat.

The time spent watching the lake fill made an impression on me. Through the years there were few, if any, good fishing spots there that I didn't know like the back of my hand.

As I pulled the car to a stop overlooking the boathouses and dock I knew exactly where I would take Savannah this afternoon for her first fishing lesson. About sixty feet to the left of an old stump, directly across the lake from the dock, was a spreading beech tree. The tree's lower branches touched the water in a semicircular fashion, protecting a large area of shady, shallow water. The tree's size suggested it was pushing its one-hundredth birthday.

At this time of year the shellcrackers and bluegills had fanned out four dozen or so beds in which their eggs had been laid and fertilized. These beds resembled foot-wide white saucers in the dark, thin water. These nurseries were jealously guarded by both parents. Any bug approaching within several feet of home was immediately engulfed by either Mom or Pop. It was here that Savannah would learn to catch fish.

I unloaded the gear, and handed Savannah the paddle, boat cushions, and fish basket. After gathering up the rods, bait, and tackle box, I led her down the brick walk and into the wide, wooden, low-ceilinged boathouse. This was where my Uncle Jim kept an aluminum boat fitted with a five-horsepower Evinrude outboard motor. No one but my uncle ever used this boat. He liked to troll for bass and never fished any other way.

Dad, Granddad, and I never trolled so there was a separate and much smaller covered area for our long, slender, handmade wooden paddle boat. It was painted porch green in color. A wonderful fishing boat, it was twelve feet long, quite narrow for its length, and it had a comfortable seat at either end. Best of all, It was very easy to paddle.

I unlocked the boat, pulled the rusty chain through the sheer, and slid the slender craft out from under its cover parallel to the low board walkway. In went the gear, and we were off in the direction of the old beech tree.

I pushed from the dock and took a couple of strokes toward our destination with the paddle. I put it across the gunwales and just let the boat drift into the middle of the flat, calm lake.

Class was now in session. I picked up the lighter and shorter of the two cane poles, and pulled the long, thin hook from the butt end where it had been stuck in the soft bamboo for safe transport. Then I rolled the pole over and over to unwind the six-pound-test monofilament line. Finally I slipped the red wooden peg from the top of the worn yellow cork and slid the cork to twelve inches above the hook. Savannah watched all this in silence.

When I had the pole all ready I said, "Here's how it works, Savannah. We're going over there toward that large beech tree with its branches in the water." With the pole I pointed toward the towering beech tree and asked, "See how the fish are moving the water under the limbs?"

"No," she answered, "I don't see where you are talking about."

"Look now, see that giant stump in the water? It's the biggest tree just to the left. See the limbs touching the water? Watch closely, and look just inside the limbs. You'll see the fish roil the water."

I pointed again, and we sat there a few moments. A big bream smacked a bug that had the misfortune of falling from the limb above. Several other fish swirled in anticipation.

"Oh! I see them now. I see them!" she said with much excitement.

"Good, now let me show you what you have to do."

I plucked a big, fat, lively cricket from the wire bait basket and threaded it onto the hook. I started the thin hook right below its head, down the length of its body, and out the rear. The cricket spat what we called tobacco juice at me as I adjusted it so that it sat perfectly and naturally on the hook. I held the line right above the hook in my left hand and the pole in my right.

"Give the pole just a gentle swinging motion, let the line go, and drop the cricket in the water wherever you want it to go."

I demonstrated. The cricket swung out and gently dropped at the end on the ten-foot line.

"Watch the cork. See how it follows the cricket? As the cricket sinks, the float follows along. When it is at the full twelve-inch depth see how the cork tips up? The fish often will hit the bait while the cricket is drifting down, so watch the cork carefully. It'll start moving faster than normal and then suddenly disappear. That's when you want to gently pull back to set the hook. Don't pull or jerk back hard. Just gently." I emphasized.

"The water's very shallow in there, so when you get one on I'm going to backpaddle. You just lead the fish out so we don't spook the rest of them. We want to catch several out of that area. When we get back away from the bream bed some, you can lead the fish over to my end of the boat, and I'll take it off and put another cricket on. Then we'll see if we can get another one."

"Think you got it?" I asked.

"I think so. Let me try," she said.

I handed her the pole and said, "Let's practice a couple of times out here in the deeper water."

Savannah took the limber pole and tried to catch the line. It swung past her, once on the left side. Then it swung once to the right, closely passing my head, and back out front. With one long reach she finally caught the line. She smiled at me in apology.

I said, "It's okay, you're doing fine. Now hold the line right above the hook and swing it out. Let go of the hook."

After three or four jerky attempts and noisy plops of the hook and cork, she began to get the feel of it.

I finally said, "That's pretty good. Let's give 'em a try. You get ready but don't go until I stop the boat and tell you when," I said.

I eased the boat forward. When I was twenty-five feet away from the closest limb, I swung the boat parallel to the bank and backpaddled once. The boat came to a gentle stop.

"Savannah, aim for the closest limb. Just ease it in there. Try not to hit a branch."

She was pretty well coordinated, and the first attempt was good, but a little short.

I said, "That's fine. Let it sit there."

I knew the hook was probably a little too far out, but that was better for the first attempt than being too far in. Savannah might get the hook hung up and spook the whole school of fish. The little, yellow cork sat a full two minutes before I told her to pick it up and try a little closer.

She did just as I told her. This time the cricket touched down within a hand's width of where the leafy twig touched the water. Instantly we saw a large swirl, and the two-inch-long yellow cork disappeared below the surface like it had been fired from a gun. Savannah's instinct took over, and she hauled back with all her strength. The big broad fish dashed under the tree, and the pole almost went double. The line cut through the water with a singing sound. As the fish got closer to the surface, it lost its advantage. Then Savannah and the limber pole won out.

The pound-size, dark purple-and-orange oval shot out from under the tree, became airborne, passed Savannah's head as she screamed, and passed my head as I ducked. It got to the end of the line some ten feet behind the boat and started back toward us. I ducked a second time, but Savannah wasn't quick enough. The broad, flat side of the fish hit her right in the forehead, nearly knocking her backward into the water. The fish slid full length down her face, down the front of her white blouse, into her lap, and finally ended up flapping around the floor of the boat. Savannah dropped to her knees, grabbed the fish in both hands, and held her prize up as she whooped and hollered.

I was laughing so hard I was not much help. At last I retrieved her trophy, gently extracted the hook, held it up one last time for her approval, and dropped it into the fish basket I had tied to the boat's right side. As I retrieved the pole and hook and rebaited it, Savannah leaned over the side of the boat, scooped a great double-handful of pond water and splashed it over her face. As the water dripped from her cheeks and nose, she leaned over once more to wash her hands in the lake. She pulled her shirttail out of her tight-fitting jeans and used it to wipe her face while exposing a lot of trim, tanned midriff. It was quite clear she was wearing nothing beneath her now soaking wet, white cotton blouse. I couldn't resist smiling, and she caught me in the act.

She glanced down at the front of her blouse, realized the cause of my reaction, and asked "What are you smiling so about?"

"Uh, uh, nice blouse," I stammered. I was concentrating as hard as I could on grabbing another cricket out of the bait bucket. I thought, *What in the world are you saying?*

In an attempt to change the subject I suggested, "Let's see if we can catch another one. But, don't jerk so hard this time. Just ease back on the line when the cork goes under. Try to keep 'em in the water."

Savannah was a quick learner and had excellent eye-hand coordination. She caught seven more really nice shellcrackers before she got a little too excited and wrapped two feet of line around one of the lower twigs. She jerked the pole back to free the line and moved the limb considerably in doing so. The water under the tree boiled as two dozen or more healthy bream spooked and headed for deeper water.

"No, no, don't pull!" I loudly whispered. "Don't spook them! Lay your pole in the water, and leave it there. It'll just float there."

She reluctantly did as I told her. I pulled back on the paddle, moving the boat twenty feet or so away from the tree. The pole floated in the water with the line tangled around the limb.

"We'll let them rest a minute" I explained. "We'll get the pole and untangle the line last thing."

As we waited for the fish to settle down, I picked up the fly rod, tied on a bright orange, foam rubber spider with six white rubber legs. I stripped forty feet of line from the reel and placed it in the bottom of the boat.

I said to her "We spooked them pretty good. The water's very shallow in there. We'll ease back up, and I'll see if I can pull a couple more out on a fly. We'll stay out further, and they may settle down."

I laid the fly rod across the gunwale, let ten feet of line and the saucy little spider trail in the water, picked up the paddle, and moved the boat so I could cast to the far left side of the bream bed. As I moved the boat, a slight breeze drifted toward us with the distinct smell of watermelon.

"Smell that?" I asked.

"What?" she said.

"Take a deep breath and tell me what you smell," I said.

She breathed in. "I don't know. It's sort of a sweet, musky smell. What is it?"

"Does it smell like watermelon to you?" I asked.

"Yes, yes, it does! What does it come from?"

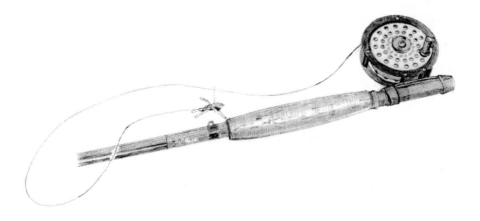

"It's the shellcrackers and bluegills. Whenever you smell that you know you are very close to their bed, usually a very large group of them. Sometimes it's the quickest way to find them when they are in deeper water."

The boat was now fifty feet from the magic spot. I brought it to a stop. I put down the paddle and picked up the well-used fly rod in my right hand and the coils of extra line in my left. After three false casts I let just enough slide through the fingers on my left hand to allow the end of the light yellow floating section to settle six feet from the outside tree limb. As the six-foot leader laid a soft loop out, it passed narrowly between two twigs, and the orange foam spider settled ten inches inside the dark shadows. I let it lie perfectly still while the small concentric circles moved out and away. I waited a slow count to ten and then barely twitched the rod tip. The spider lightly danced on its rubber legs then disappeared in a mini-explosion. I pulled my left hand back, setting the hook as the big female shellcracker headed in the opposite direction.

"Holy cow!" Savannah cried.

I took the line in my right hand and held tight against the stained cork grip of the rod. A large bow in the rod kept the line tight. I grabbed the paddle with my left hand so that I could pull the boat and fish away from the tree and the rest of the school. I played the big bream and enjoyed feeling the line cut through the warm summer water. Two minutes later I lifted the biggest shellcracker of the day over the shallow gunwale. It was so broad I couldn't get my hands around it, so I pinned it to the boat bottom with one hand and slid the hook out of its lip with the other. I held the fish up, and we both admired its glistening golds, greens, and blacks in the strong late afternoon light. It was one of the biggest of the season and must have weighed twice as much as any that Savannah had caught.

"Holy cow!" Savannah said again. "That was beautiful! What a fish! I want to learn how to catch them with a fly rod. Will you show me how to use one of those?"

"Sure, we'll practice. You can learn to cast a fly rod. No problem." I promised. "It's getting late though. Watch me, and I'll try to catch a couple more right quick. That'll give you and your granddad enough for a meal."

I repeated the performance twice more, and we were back at the dock as dusk settled over the narrow valley. As I was cleaning the ten fat bream for the frying pan, we heard a huge splash and both looked up in time to see a very large fish boiling the shallow water behind the big stump. For a full five minutes that monster plowed through the grass with a third of its wide back out of the water, stirring up mud with its strong tail and scattering half-grown bream in all directions. From all the way across the lake I knew it had to be him, the same giant bass I had seen the night before.

Even to Savannah's inexperienced eye, the big fish was impressive.

"Holy cow!" she said for the third time that day. "Johnny, let's catch that one."

"No, no, not tonight," I said, knowing full well that nobody was going to be casting to that fish but me. That one was to be all mine. Besides I thought it was going to be hard as heck to get that old boy to bite. The spot he was feeding in was almost impossible to reach without spooking such a big experienced fish.

As I finished scaling and gutting the bream, the old lunker made one more lunge through the shallows. We could only hear him now. It was too dark to see him glide back into the three feet of dark, cool water right behind the big oak stump. Savannah stood and rinsed off the fish in the lake water as I handed them to her and dropped the dripping, now scaleless, cleaned fish back into the wire basket.

She stood up, wiped her hands on the legs of her jeans and said, "That was so much fun. Thanks for bringing me."

"I enjoyed it too," I said. "You did really well. Your grandfather's going to be very impressed," I said as I held up the basket. "It's pretty late. Let's get you back to town."

We divided up the gear. Savannah wanted to carry the fish, so we added them to her half of the equipment and headed up the steep walk. I started the car and turned on the lights so we could see. I lowered the station wagon's tailgate. I spread out several sheets of the weekend newspaper to set the fish on and slid the fly rod and cane poles over the backseat and front seat, resting the butt ends on the dashboard.

As we went to get in, I noticed a huge spider web caught in the beam of the headlights. Seeing such a big, fresh web formed at this time of night meant beautiful fair weather the next day. I could not resist.

"Come around the front of the car, and let me show you something," I told Savannah.

As she came around I led her to the large, symmetrical web, making her stand to one side so the light from the car beam would not be blocked.

"When you see a new web like that you know it's going to be a good fishing day the next day. The spider knows not to go to all that hard work if the rain and wind are coming," I said.

"It's beautiful. I've never seen one so perfect," she said.

I pointed to the upper left-hand section, almost two feet from the tightly woven center and almost out of the light. There was the master builder and hunter. Almost two inches of black and yellow, its body was as large as the end of my little finger.

"Watch this." I grabbed the first big moth that passed in front of the bright beams and threw the fluttering creature against the center of the web. The instant the moth touched the web the hungry spider raced down the silky strands and covered the moth with more sticky silk threads. The moth stopped moving in seconds.

"Holy cow," Savannah whispered.

We retraced our path back up to the gate, careful to unlock and relock it, and I had her home by ten o'clock. I sent her inside to get a big bowl. When she returned, I pushed open the spring-loaded bottom of the wire fish basket and let her first mess of fish slide into the bowl. She looked down at the full bowl in the light of the single bulb hanging above the porch, then up at me.

"Thank you, I had a wonderful time," she said. She slipped her right hand behind my neck, pulled me toward her slightly, and kissed me. This was not a peck on the cheek by my Aunt Laura. I thought I was never going to get to breathe again. For the first time in my life, here I was being kissed by a very beautiful girl and I had met her only eleven hours before.

Holy cow!

As she stepped back slightly, I finally remembered to breathe, and I blurted out "You wanna practice that some more tomorrow?"

Savannah laughed out loud.

I stammered, "No, I mean would you like to go practice fishing some more tomorrow?"

She answered, "That sounds like great fun!" She then cocked her head slightly, smiled, and said "Yes, let's do try that some more tomorrow."

On the short drive home, the warm summer night flooded through the open windows. The tingle of my first real kiss held a big smile on my face. My thought was, *Yes, sir, there's the record-breaking bass to catch, but this summer there may be bigger fish to fry.*

NEVER A BIGGER FISH TO FRY

PART TWO

Next morning I was at my summer job by 7:45 A.M. I was working at the glass plant on the first shift, from 8:00 A.M. to 4:00 P.M. that included one ten-minute break at 9:15 A.M., fifteen minutes at noon for lunch, and ten minutes at 2:30 P.M. for the afternoon break. I was working with a school buddy in the wash area. Both our fathers had worked full time at the plant for years, giving us first shot at the summer job openings. Because of the limited number of good jobs in our town, that connection served as the surest way that our town had to offer for a young person to make enough money for a college education.

Johnny Walker and I were assigned the task of washing the misprinted labels off of the Coca-Cola bottles. This was a very hot, boring, production line-paced job. I was very glad to have a companion helping alongside. Otherwise, I think I would have lost my mind.

By 4:30 P.M. Monday afternoon I was home and in and out of the shower. I put the crickets left over from yesterday back in the car, and it was off to pick up Savannah. Again she was right on time, and we arrived at the lake by 5:30 P.M. As I began to unload the car, I picked up the cricket basket. Savannah asked what we needed them for.

I said, "So you can catch some fish."

"No," she replied, "I want to catch them on the fly rod like you did yesterday. I want to learn to do it that way."

"You did very good with the crickets yesterday. You sure you don't want to do it that way again?" I asked.

"No," she said, "I really liked doing it that way. It was wonderful fun, but I want to learn the way you were doing it."

I placed the cricket bucket in the shade of the closest tree as I answered, "Okay, but it'll take practice. You won't catch as many fish 'til you know more about it."

Savannah said, "I don't care how many I catch, I just want to learn to do it well with a fly rod."

Leaving the two cane poles in the car, we started for the boathouse and dock. I didn't even unlock the boat, but took the fly rod and Savannah out on the long wooden dock. At the end of the walkway was a floating section that remained only twelve inches above the water line.

We got to the very end and the lesson began. I stripped out about ten feet of line and pulled the leader to me. I cut off the little rubber spider that I had used the afternoon before so we would not have to worry about the sharp hook during lesson one.

"Savannah, you stand on my left side and watch me first," I said. She moved over as I took one small single coil of line in my left hand and began to move the rod tip back and forward, back and forward.

"Watch the rod tip," I instructed. "Back and forward. It's the same motion as if you were painting a ceiling with the rod tip. Back, then forward. Always pretending you are painting a ceiling.

Never letting the rod tip leave the surface you are painting. If you go too far forward you lose contact with the ceiling. If you move the tip too far back you lose touch with the ceiling. Backward, stop, forward, stop." I demonstrated several more times. "Now you try it."

We switched places. I gave her the rod and she began to cast. As expected, too far back, and too far forward at first.

I said, "Now watch your rod tip. Stop going forward at about ten o'clock and stop your back cast at two o'clock." She began again. Better this time. Painting the imaginary ceiling. Ten o'clock, two o'clock; a little smoother each time.

After about fifteen minutes of practice I let out ten more feet of line and said, "Now try using a little more line."

She began her back cast but stopped and said, "I think I would get the correct rhythm down quicker if you would hold my wrist and show me where to start and stop."

I thought about the logistics of this for a split second, walked up behind her, carefully stretched around with my right hand to take her right wrist. I found I had to move very close to reach around. When I did, Savannah leaned back slightly and I found my face almost buried in her wonderfully long hair. Now our entire bodies were touching. In the heat of the June afternoon, this simple innocent act sent my pulse racing through my whole being. It was a sensation I had not known before.

I quickly lost all thought of fishing lessons. For the life of me I could not figure out what to do with my left hand, so I stuck it in the left pocket of my jeans.

This turned out to be a bad idea, as in doing so I inadvertently brushed along some other parts of Savannah's anatomy. Realizing where my hand was, I jerked it out of my pocket. The safest place remaining seemed to be the upper part of her left arm. As I stood there holding her to me, I was trying really hard to remember what it was I was supposed to be doing. At that moment Savannah turned her head, looked over her shoulder and into my eyes. With a laughing smile she said, "Are we ready yet?"

I wasn't sure about her selection of the pronoun we, but blurted out, "I certainly am!"

I thought, *What in the world are you saying!*

And I quickly added, "Yes, I think we can continue. Just relax your right arm and follow my lead." I moved her wrist back, elbow close to her side, stopped at about two o'clock, waited a second to let the rod load and pushed her wrist forward. We did this for half a dozen casts.

Each time I guided less and let her have more control. She was a quick learner.

"Now you try by yourself," I began.

"That's good," I encouraged. "That's much better."

"Now," I instructed, "start again and this time on your forward cast, speed up, stop sharply, and let the extra line in your left hand go."

Savannah did just as I had instructed and the whole line laid out and lit gently on the water. Picture perfect!

She did this very well for ten or fifteen more casts.

It was time to try the real thing.

"Savannah, you're ready. Let's see if we can find a fish."

I sensed her enthusiasm and excitement as I turned to unlock the boat.

It was right at dusk. The fading light was perfect for fishing topwater flies. Savannah would still be able to see where her line and fly were going, and this would help her get better with each cast. About halfway down the right side of the lake a nice one-pound bass smashed her popping bug. Between her whoops and hollers I was able to coach her through landing her first bass. When I got the hook out, I handed her the little trophy. She held it in both hands, turned it around, looked at it eyeball to eyeball for a second, kissed it right on its lips, and then gently slid it back into the dark warm water.

As she brought her hand out of the water she splashed a handful right in my face, laughed, and said, "Not bad for a beginner, huh? Can we try for one more before dark?" she begged.

Savannah flashed a smile that I would have said yes to no matter the request. I turned the boat toward the left side of the lake, and we worked that bank on the way back toward the boathouse.

Savannah missed two more good strikes but her casting was improving. As we approached the big stump just across the lake from the boathouse, I intentionally started to pull away and head in. I, in no way, wanted Savannah, or anyone else for that matter, to be flailing around the haunts of my record breaking bass. As we headed to the boathouse, my back was to the stump and Savannah was facing it. Even in the growing darkness I could see the surprise in her eyes before I heard the tremendous splash made by the big bass as he completed a successful attack on some unsuspecting prey. I turned in time to see the water fold down over his huge body.

"Holy cow!" was all Savannah could muster.

I thought, *I know, I know. He's big, really big!*

I docked and locked the boat and we carried the equipment up to the car. As I put the rod in the back and closed up the rear of the station wagon I said, "You did very well today. You'll be a pro in no time."

She replied, "I really want to get good at this. Can we keep doing the lessons?"

I thought, *Don't throw this rabbit in the briar patch.*

"Sure," I replied, "I don't have anything else to do after work most days. I'd like to teach you."

"So can we come tomorrow?" she asked.

"Of course, I'll pick you up at the same time."

"Thank you for being so patient. You're a really good teacher."

She reached up in the fading light, stood on her tiptoes, and again kissed me. This time I tried to kiss her back. When she finally pulled gently away, she smiled and said, "I think I can teach you some things too. Want to swap lessons?"

I said, "I believe I would like that very much."

With a peck on the cheek she added, "Then it's a deal."

As I went around the car I heard the telltale sound of that big old bass plowing through the shallows, terrorizing everything in or near the old oak stump. I would be back in the morning, just before the sun came up.

5:30 A.M. found me quietly unlocking the boat. It had showered sometime during the night, and small drops of moisture were still dripping off the willow trees as I slid the boat out of its slip. I laid the green boat cushion on the damp seat, quietly put the fly rod on the bottom of the boat with tip balanced on the gunwale, and pushed off silently toward the opposite shore. I let the boat drift as I ran my fingers over the ten-pound leader. Feeling one wind knot and a rough place or two caused me to cut the whole thing off and tie on a new leader. To the end I attached a Peck's popping bug that was pure black with black feathers covering an unusually long shank hook. The big bug imitation had two thin white lines painted down each side, blood-red eyes with white circles around them. The Peck's Popper was one of the most deadly big bass flies I had ever used.

Now as I sat perfectly still in the boat, I could hear fish rising all up and down the lake in the mist of dawn. I knew it was going to be a good morning. I could feel it. But I did not have much time. I had to be at work by 7:45 A.M. so I only had about an hour. I eased the boat in the direction of the oak stump. I was watching the surface of the water around the stump for a push to see if the big bass I was after would begin feeding.

I was pretty close now to casting distance, paddle in hand, just watching. I sat there for a full fifteen minutes. Good fish were rising around me and I was tempted to move and just start catching fish. But the sheer size of the fish I had caught sight of two nights before was more than enough to keep me waiting. I was sure I had seen the largest bass I would probably ever see.

I would wait.

Another few minutes more passed. There it was! A slight movement of water directly behind the stump. I could not see what caused it, but the ripples moved out from either side. The movement seemed a little more to the right, so I decided to cast to that side.

I false casted two times, letting out enough line to load up the five-weight rod. Then I dropped the popper just to the right of the stump and about six inches past. I saw, back in among the grass, the fish slightly move its huge tail. I had missed it earlier, but I now saw it move left, then right, slowly advancing in the shallow water toward my fly – which lay dead still. My heart was beating fifteen beats to the dozen as the fish picked up speed.

He had bought the lie.

The water here was very shallow and the fish was big. It made a considerable push as it approached. The adrenaline rush kicked in as the distance closed. Just then a fifteen-pound hole appeared in the glassy smooth surface. The bass had inhaled the popper.

Simultaneously I pulled the line tight with my left hand and raised the rod tip to set the razor sharp hook. I might just as well have set the hook in the oak stump – nothing moved. Not an inch.

For a split second I thought, *I'm hung up on the darn stump!*

Then the line went completely slack giving me near heart failure. Was the fish on or off? In less than a blink of an eye the pond exploded as the bass became completely airborne. Reaching the apex of its jump, it opened its mouth and with blood-red gills flaring, shook its entire body in a violent rage. For a split second my popper was tightly lodged in its jug-size jaw. Then the Peck's Popper came loose and shot toward me following a final vicious shake of his head.

The popper hit the side of the boat with a loud whop! The bass crashed back below the surface, and the gaping hole in the lake sealed over as spreading concentric rings warped the reflection of the dawn's morning sky.

The trembling started. I just sat there looking into space where the old lunker still hung airborne in my minds' eye. My hands were shaking. I laid the rod across the gunwale of the boat, leaned forward with my elbows on my knees and ran the brief encounter over and over in my mind.

I do not know how many minutes passed, but my thoughts were broken as a glimpse of my black Peck's Popper floating by the boat caught my eye. I took up the paddle, scooped it under the faux bug and drew it to me.

I picked it off the paddle blade, shook off the water and examined it. The hook had miraculously held, but the rear black feathers were a wreck. Five of the six white rubber legs were missing and the paint job was only a memory.

Somehow I made it to work on time.

During my fifteen-minute lunch break I called Savannah at her grandfather's house to see if she still wanted to do something after I got off work. Her answer was "Yes, of course. Can we go back to the lake again?"

I was glad that she wanted to go. We set the time and it was back to the wash rack.

Off at four, quick few minutes to the house, in the shower, clean shirt and jeans, told Mom I was going fishing and leave me some supper on the stove. Gone!

Savannah was closing the front porch door behind her as I drove up. She took the steps two at a time, opened the car back door, put in a small red metal cooler that had Coca-Cola written in script down its sides, and slid in the front seat.

"Are we going to the bait place?" she asked.

"If you want to fish with the crickets, I still have some," I said. Their incessant chirping confirmed their location in the rear of the station wagon.

"We really don't need them this afternoon if you are going to use the fly rod," I explained.

"Good, but we need to stop so we can pick up some beer," Savannah said.

I thought quickly. *There was no we to this idea. I had never bought a beer, wasn't old enough to buy one, had never tasted one, and sure as heck would be reported by our efficient small town grapevine to Mom if seen even buying beer. No, that risk was too great even to please Savannah. Savannah was going to have to deal with the beer.*

With some reluctance and embarrassment I explained this situation to my new, much more worldly, fishing partner.

Savannah took the news in stride. If she thought this incredible, at least she was kind enough not to laugh. She said, "Well, can you take us by somewhere that I can buy a few bottles for the cooler? I can go in and get it. I have my own money."

I quickly thought of all the places that were off-limits to me and my school friends. The Hub Drive-in popped to the top of the list so I headed there. It was but a half-mile out of the way.

At 5:15 P.M. on a Monday there was not much yet going on at the Hub. It was creatively built in a circular fashion, thus its name. I was grateful that the parking lot circumvented the building, allowing me the opportunity to ease the station wagon around the rear out of sight. The facts that you could buy beer, no questions asked, and park out of sight seemed to be attractive features at the Hub as demonstrated by large teenage crowds every weekend.

As I pulled to a stop, Savannah jumped out of the car, walked across the rear gravel parking area, and returned shortly with a brown paper sack that she carried with one hand supporting the bottom. She opened the rear door on her side and withdrew six longneck amber bottles, sweating from their ice-cold contents. The seventh bottle she extracted was a twelve-ounce Dr. Pepper.

Savannah placed five of the longnecks in the double-walled cooler and deftly popped the cap off one.

"Hold this," she said as she passed me the beer. She then repeated the procedure with the Dr. Pepper bottle, closed the rear door, hopped in the front seat, switched cola for beer, and took a long swig. She lowered the bottle, looked at me, and flashed that smile. "I think I'm ready."

We drove to the farm, windows down, hair blowing in the breeze. I stole a glance at her and thought, *I'm in way over my head here. Butter in a hot frying pan has more of a chance.*

I continued working first shift at Laurens Glass, now stitching up cardboard shipping boxes for Mount Olive Pickle jars. During the next couple of weeks Savannah and I settled into a pleasant routine. She landed the 6 A.M.–to-late-lunch job as a waitress at the Toasty Grill Café. The word I got was the breakfast and lunch business had doubled, and the early morning all-male coffee club had to move to a much bigger table. It did not surprise me one bit. Savannah was a strikingly beautiful, eighteen-year-old woman.

On my fifteen-minute lunch break I would drop a dime into the pay phone and dial Toasty Grill's number, 735, and check to see if she wanted to meet at the farm.

The answer was always an enthusiastic "Yes!"

After our second week I made Savannah her own key for the lake gate. She had found a place she could buy beer in Watts Mill which was on the way to the farm.

After she got off work she would drive her grandfather's 1952 Plymouth out and wait for me. Savannah would beat me there by about an hour or so. I usually found her on the dock, two beers into a six-pack, stretched out on an old green bedspread that she had found at her grandfather's and now carried regularly in her car. I learned very quickly that Savannah had brought with her to the United States several European ideas. One was her wardrobe and the other how much of it she might, or might not, wear. At age 14, except in very risqué and controversial Spring-maid calendar ads, I had never seen a girl in a two-piece outfit. Savannah had such a thing. When not sunbathing she actually wore both pieces. Hearing my car coming down the dirt path, she would meet me at the boathouse door to help with the gear. She had become a very avid fisherman and was always ready to practice her fly casting. As the fly-fishing lessons continued, Savannah was becoming darn good. She had that natural delicate touch. As the days got longer and the lake water hotter, we started fishing different methods as the fish had moved to deep cool water. She became good at them all and seemed to never tire of catching even the smallest fish.

I must say, if Savannah was enjoying learning to fish, I was equally enjoying the experience she was bringing to the closing minutes of those warm summer nights. As the days wore on, pay-back kissing lessons moved from the dock to the front seat of her grandfather's spacious Plymouth.

For weeks I had been burning the candle at both ends. By late July I was about to give up entirely on the big bass. Savannah and I were spending four or five afternoons and evenings at the farm. I would get home late and be back at the farm by 5:00 A.M. to 5:30 A.M. and then work all day. The hot weather, it seemed, had driven the old rascal to deep water. I had not seen a sign of him in days. So I cut back on my morning trips and just enjoyed being with Savannah.

One Saturday afternoon late in July, Savannah and I had rendezvoused mid-morning at the lake. We fished until around two o'clock. We ate a picnic lunch that Savannah had put up, and were just sitting there on the dock with our feet dangling in the water. Savannah, with a little buzz on from a couple of beers and the warm sun, was laughing at some story I was telling her when low and behold my Uncle Jim came down the brick walk toward the boathouse. This surprised me. Although my uncle liked to fish, we had not seen him all summer here at the lake. I quickly headed up the dock to the boathouse to meet him. As he started out of the boathouse, I met him and said, "Uncle Jim, can I help you get your fishing gear out of your car?"

Looking over my head and down the dock at Savannah, he said, "No, no, it's alright. I'm just going to pick up the outboard motor today."

I looked in the direction of his stare and said, "Do you know Mr. Ashburn's granddaughter, Savannah? She's here visiting for the summer."

Never taking his eyes off her, he said, "No, we've not met."

Savannah did not move. Just continuing to dangle her feet in the water and, sipping on her beer, she never even looked in our direction.

I said, "Let me help you."

"No," my uncle said, "I just need to get the motor off. I'm taking it to McDaniel's to get it serviced."

I helped him get the motor off the transom of the aluminum trolling boat and carried it up to his car. Even though the Evinrude was only five horsepower it was very heavy. As Uncle Jim opened the trunk to his Plymouth, he looked down on the dock once more. Savannah turned, looked up, and gave one of her million dollar smiles. Uncle Jim looked across the top of the car at me and raised both eyebrows. He said, "Have a good time. See you tomorrow morning." Uncle Jim was my Sunday School teacher. He had in his class a group of nine fourteen-year-old boys. All of us were school buddies.

When I got back to the dock I sat back down close to Savannah and stuck my bare feet back in the lake. The water was, as all lakes are, layers of warm, then cold, then warm again. It is an unusual sensation. I touched my foot to hers and pulled it slowly up her calf. She laughed, jumped up and said, "Let's go catch a fish, big boy. Your lesson doesn't start for another couple hours," she teased.

The wait was worth it. When I followed Savannah home that night I whispered a small prayer, "Lord don't let this summer ever end."

I didn't sleep well that night. I kept wondering if Uncle Jim would say anything about me being with Savannah at the farm and, if so, would my parents think anything of it. Worrying aside, the next morning with my parents and two younger sisters, I was at Sunday School on time.

I must confess I wasn't paying much attention to the lesson Uncle Jim was teaching until I heard the words, "heavy petting". All my friends' heads popped up. Was the timing and subject of this lesson just a coincidence? I wondered. Uncle Jim was explaining the dangers that heavy petting could lead to.

As he described the pitfalls I thought, *So that's what grownups call it.*

As the lesson got a little more graphic, I noticed all my friends were studying their shoes with great interest. Mine too became a growing curiosity and looked like they needed re-tying.

Both of them. It was an insufferably long hour, however I learned a lot. I now knew what I was enjoying so much had a name. It was clear that grownups had sufficient personal experience with this and that such actions could have some pitfalls. This also confirmed in my mind what I already had discovered: it was the best thing I ever had tried!

As Uncle Jim closed the lesson, he looked straight at me and said, and I'm paraphrasing, "Just remember, vertical and in the light is alright, horizontal in the dark is a big problem."

Sunday afternoon, Monday, and Tuesday, passed without my parents saying a word about the amount of time I was spending at the farm. I kept meeting Savannah there, but I was still worried about my uncle knowing who I was spending so much time with. Might my uncle still say something to Mom or Dad?

Wednesday was as hot as blue blazes. By the time I got to the farm it was clear Savannah had cooled off with a swim. It was not the first time she had embraced the skinny-dipping idea. Throughout our summer swims Savannah had teased me because I would never take off my tighty-whities. After my Uncle Jim's Sunday School lesson I had made up my mind that no matter what, those were not coming off.

When I got down to the dock she was dressed – well mostly. She had on this two-piece outfit that she looked terrific in and was sitting on the edge of the dock with a lot of tan midriff showing. She was wringing the water out of her long hair which shone like a raven's wing in the hot sun. About that time Uncle Jim appeared. He came down to the boathouse and headed out on the adjoining dock. He was carrying the freshly tuned-up Evinrude motor and a two-gallon galvanized can of gasoline.

As he walked down the dock where his boat was tied, I was

watching from the other dock and could tell the exact instant he spied Savannah. He never took his eyes off her, that is, not until he walked right off the end of the dock, motor, gas can, and all. For a moment it was as if he was suspended in midair; then there was this spectacular splash. Only his cap was left floating on the surface.

Savannah jumped up and we both raced down the dock into the boathouse and out on the adjoining dock where Uncle Jim had disappeared. Luckily the water at that end of the dock was only five feet deep. By the time we got to him Uncle Jim had gained his footing on the muddy bottom. He was spitting and sputtering, but he was unhurt. We both knelt down on the very end of the dock and reached out to help. We liked to have never gotten him out because he refused to let go of the heavy motor or the gas can. He was just standing there, neck deep, still holding on to them. He finally passed me the motor and then the gas can, which made it possible for Savannah and me to pry him out of the mud and help him back toward land and up the slippery bank.

After we got him dried off some, retrieved his cap from the lake, and got the waterlogged motor back into the trunk of his car, I was pretty certain Mom and Dad were not going to find out about Savannah from Uncle Jim.

Saved!

One afternoon in early August I arrived at the farm at the usual time. As I started down the winding steep brick walk to the boathouse, I could see Savannah sitting on the step to the float-ing dock. She wore navy-blue shorts, and her long dark hair fell over a white cotton blouse. Her darkly tanned skin glowed in the late afternoon sun. Even from a hundred feet away she was stun-ningly beautiful.

As I got to her side she never even turned. She was holding a letter and crying. Not knowing what to do or say, I put the fly rod down and just sat down beside her. I handed her my handkerchief. In a few minutes she began to get herself together. Drying her eyes she took a long swallow from the beer sitting beside her and said, "I'm sorry, I don't feel like a fishing lesson today."

We just sat there in the gathering dusk. After a while she said, "You don't know why I'm here in the States, do you?"

"Just to spend the summer with your grandfather, I thought," I offered.

"It's not like that. My father made me come here; here to be away from a man I was seeing back in Italy. He's a sergeant in the army, and he was my father's driver. We were falling in love and even talked about getting married. My father forbade me seeing him, but I kept on. So he sent me here. This letter's from Brad, my boyfriend. He says he has just been reassigned as a military adviser to a place called Vietnam on a four-year tour. Brad writes that it's over. He doesn't think he'll make it back. He says we'll never see each other again. Even if we could, my father will never let us be together. Brad's right, of course, I'll never be free to be with him again," she whispered and began to sob softly. I held her close until she had cried it out and then I followed her home.

Savannah didn't take my calls for two days. But by the third day I was really ready to see her, so I took another chance and called the café. The other waitress that worked from lunch 'til closing answered the phone, "Toasty Grill Café, can I help you?"

Gladys, at sixty years old and pushing three hundred pounds, had a voice that any army drill sergeant at Fort Jackson would have given his eye teeth for. I knew what was coming next. At the level of an air horn on a Mack truck, she hollered, "Savannah, it's that boy again." I winced and held my breath.

I knew Al Rawls, the owner, probably did not like me calling during Savannah's working hours, but with the crowds she was drawing I wasn't too worried.

When Savannah answered, I said, "How about a fishing lesson?"

"You're on. Meet you after work," she whispered and hung up.

We had a great time that afternoon. For whatever reason the subject of Brad never came up again, and we picked up where we had left off.

A couple weeks later something very unusual happened. It actually cooled off a little. It felt wonderful. The humidity, like the temperature, dropped a little and I started back fishing for my big bass early in the mornings. My hunch was right and on the second morning out I saw the old rascal had moved back into his shallow water haunt behind the barrel-size stump.

On two separate mornings, one week apart, the bass struck the tempting imitation fat black bug, but in both cases went around the stump and broke off the ten-pound leader. It was clear from these two attempts that the only way to catch this fellow was to hook him, stand up in the boat, and hold the rod high enough to keep the line from touching the stump. At the same time I needed to move the boat far enough away from the stump to clear the line. This was not going to happen with just one person. Of this I was now convinced.

August stayed relatively cool for two weeks. The fish were hitting the top water flies again, and Savannah was having a ball. We fished every evening and I was amazed at how far she had progressed during the summer with her casting. She was really quite good, and I encouraged her by often telling her so.

On August 26, the moon was just a couple days before full and as it balanced on the tip of a tall pine across the lake, it was almost as light as day. Savannah had caught some nice two-pounders and we were now, at ten o'clock, stretched out on her old green spread just enjoying the cool summer night. She was cradled in my right arm, head snuggled up in my neck. We were not saying a word, just listening to the cicadas singing and the bullfrogs croaking.

All of a sudden Savannah sat up so fast it frightened me. "It's him! I heard him!" she said.

I immediately sat up, too. From across the pond the big bass was taking apart the shallows. I had missed it at first, but there was no denying it now, it was him.

"Let's go," Savannah said. She was on her feet. "You can catch him tonight. Let's go," she insisted.

I listened to him tearing up the patch. He was definitely in a feeding frenzy. The boat was still tied up. Rod ready. "Okay," I said. "Let's go." We piled in and I quickly paddled across the lake. I knew that handling the boat was the key to catching the big fish, but Savannah was not practiced at this.

About halfway across I said, "Savannah pick up the rod." In the moonlight I could see the shock on her face.

"No, it's your fish," she insisted. "You've been after him all summer. Besides, he's way too much fish for me."

"Pick up the rod, Savannah," I said. "He can only be caught if we do this together. Listen carefully to me now. You can do this. I am going to show you how. Just do as I say. I'm going to scull as quietly as possible right up to the front of that stump and turn so you will be facing the bank. That way you will be casting over your right shoulder."

"I want you to cast over the top of the stump. Pretend it's not even there. Your target is three feet behind the stump. When I square you off to the bank, you'll need to false cast once and then let the fly settle behind the stump. You won't be able to see your fly, and part of your line will be lying on top of the stump. At that point, don't move a muscle. Just wait. We won't be able to see him strike, but we will be able to hear it. When I tell you to stand up, pull your line tight with your left hand and set the hook. As soon as he is hooked I'm going to move the boat down and away from the stump. Get your line on the reel as quickly as possible and let the drag do the work. Just do as I say. Now pick up the rod and get ready."

"Are you sure you want me to try this?" she asked. "We'll only get one chance. He's not fed this hard in days."

"I'm sure. It's the only way. I want you to catch him," I said.

As we eased across the lake she cast a couple of times into the night to be sure the line was clear. She coiled the excess line in her left hand and left fifteen feet of line floating on the water.

Now I was there. I started turning the boat. She false cast over the stump aiming about four feet over its surface and as she began bringing her fly rod back, I back paddled, pulling the boat to a complete stop. The black Peck's popping bug sailed over the stump and landed like a feather halfway between the back of the stump and the bank.

We held our breath. A full minute passed. Savannah glanced over at me, and I put my finger to my lips. She turned back and gripped the rod a little tighter as she held three coils of spare line tight in her left hand. The second minute ticked by and still not a ripple. I was beginning to doubt my whole strategy.

Then it happened.

I actually saw water flying over the top of the stump before I heard the eruption. "Hit 'im!" I hollered.

Savannah pulled her left hand back as far as she could and raised her rod tip in perfect unison. She stood up in the bow of the boat. I took a big bite in the lake with the paddle, sending the boat forward and almost dumping Savannah into the drink! She was quick as a cat, got her balance, and erased the old brute's first run by releasing the three coils of line in her left hand.

Her height and the fact she was holding the fly rod as high over head as she could, combined with the forward motion of the boat, helped to clear the line from over the stump. The fight was on! No sooner than Savannah had her line on the reel, the bass cleared the water by a foot. My stomach threw a half hitch at the sight of him. Great gosh a'mighty! He was gigantic, eye busting big! Splashing down he pulled twenty feet of line off the reel, the handle knocking Savannah's knuckles with every turn.

"Sit back down, Savannah. He's hooked good, and we've got him in deep water. I don't want you falling out."

"Johnny, tell me what to do!" she said, out of breath.

"Just let him run when he wants to, but keep your rod tip up and your line tight. When he comes toward the boat, reel fast to take out the slack, but when he jumps or turns to run, take your hand quickly off the reel handles. Just let him go."

The fish was so big he was now pulling the boat around. I was working hard to keep us away from the bank and any snags as best I could. The fourth time the bass jumped, I noticed he only made it out of the water halfway.

I said, "Savannah, he's starting to tire a little, but don't let up on him. Keep that line tight, but be ready if he runs. Make him earn every inch of line."

She was really doing a great job. She was listening to my coaching and doing just what I told her to do. Savannah never let

the rod tip down. She had to be getting tired, but brother, was the adrenaline pumping! We were both breathing fast and hard.

He ran twice more and then charged the boat. When I saw him change direction for the boat, I shouted, "Savannah, reel! Reel fast, honey!"

About the time she caught up with him he ran straight under the boat, putting a horrific bend in the rod. "Stand up Savannah, and stick the tip of your rod straight down into the water!" I shouted.

She made it just at the last second. The rod held, the line held, and when he came back out from under the boat he was hers. Dead tired he let her lead him close to the rear of the boat. We had forgotten the net so I got on my knees, leaned over the gunwale, and grabbed him by the lower lip. I could not believe his size. When I hefted him over the side and held him dripping wet he looked as big as a July watermelon. No doubt a record. For sure a state record. He was magnificent!

"Savannah, you did it, you did it!" In a flood of relief she began to cry and laugh, all at the same time.

"Savannah, I'm telling you this is a record fish. I'll bet you anything he's at least a new South Carolina state record. Let's get back to the dock and find some certified scales. Somebody must still be open somewhere that's got some."

"No," she said.

"No? What do you mean 'no'?" I said.

Savannah said, "I want to turn him loose."

"You want to do what?" I asked in disbelief.

"I want to put him back. Now. Before he dies."

"Savannah, honey, this is the biggest largemouth bass caught in the history of South Carolina. I guarantee it," I pleaded.

"I don't care. Let's turn him loose, Johnny. Please. I really want him to go free," she begged.

"Savannah, are you real sure? Are you really sure? Honey, this is a once in a lifetime fish!"

"I'm sure. Let's put him back."

I held him up in the moonlight one last time, shook my head, and eased him back into the warm lake water. I just held him there for several minutes, sliding him back and forth, forcing water through his gills. As we watched him regain his strength, I could swear he was looking up into our faces with those dark eyes. Finally, I could feel him pushing against my grip with that huge tail and as I released him, he flipped his tail and soaked us both. With water dripping off Savannah's nose, we both laughed.

"Thank you, Johnny. Thank you for letting me catch him and most of all, thank you for letting him go free."

When I called the café mid-morning the next day, Gladys said Savannah was not there. I thought this strange so I called her grandfather's home. Savannah answered it on the first ring.

With great relief at hearing her voice, I asked, "Savannah, will you meet me after work today?"

"Johnny, I can't today. Will you do me a favor?"

"Sure, what is it?" I said.

"Can you get off work tomorrow and take me to Greenwood?"

"Savannah, yes, but what's in Greenwood?"

"I need to go to the airport. Johnny, I have to go home," she said.

"Home?" I asked.

"Yes, my dad sent a telegram saying it was time for me to come back to Italy. Will you take me to Greenwood?"

"Sure, Savannah. I'll take a sick day. When is your flight?"

"Johnny, how long will it take us to drive to Greenwood?"

The airport is not far after you cross over the lake. "I'd say we better leave ninety minutes ahead to be safe."

"Then pick me up at 9:00 A.M. Okay?"

As always, she was right on time. I helped her put her single bag in the back of the station wagon. She ran back up the steps and gave her grandfather a big hug. I waved to Mr. Ashburn as she slid in the passenger side.

When we arrived at the little terminal at the Greenwood Municipal Airport, I carried her bag and followed her to the counter. She paid $18.00 cash for her ticket to Atlanta. The Piedmont Airlines plane would make one stop in Athens, Georgia, and then on to Atlanta. She would make the connection on Pan Am to New York and then to Italy.

The Piedmont DC-3 was sitting on the tarmac with one engine running as we left the terminal.

As we stood waiting to be told to board, I said, "Savannah, I had no idea you had to leave. Why didn't you tell me?"

"I didn't know myself until my father sent word a week ago." She then fell into my arms and whispered into my ear, "I thought it was better this way."

When she finally pushed away from our long goodbye kiss, laughing through tears, she said, "Hey, I'd say I did a pretty good teaching job, too. Now go and see if you can find that old bass."

On the top step into the rear of the plane she turned and waved, ducked into the door, and was gone. As the plane lifted off I just stood there, both hands in my pockets, warm tears running down and dripping off my chin.

That was fifty-seven years ago. I never saw or heard from Savannah again and try as I might, there was never a bigger fish to fry!

A LOT OF BULL!

Rabon Creek was a teenager's duck-hunting dream. It meandered through the rolling county of Laurens, South Carolina, and coursed under picturesque one-lane steel bridges. When flooded, it backed up in marshy cow pastures but shared its path with numerous acorn-covered sandbars when at normal level. Rabon was not an intimidating river like the Reedy. It was not only wide enough to attract both big ducks, blacks and mallards, and, of course, many resident wood ducks, but also shallow enough to wade in freezing weather – naked to the waist – to retrieve a precious downed prize. My hunting buddy, Sammy, and I hunted Rabon Creek often.

Our most productive method was what we called cutting off the curves. Rabon Creek had abundant twists and turns as the result of the hilly land that comprised our county. It gave the area I grew up in a wonderful diverse character.

As young boys, our duck hunting did not in any way resemble that depicted by bait and bullet artists on the Winchester calendars or in national sporting magazines of the 1940s. There was no sitting in well-constructed comfortable blinds overlooking vast waterfowl-rich rice fields or shooting a hundred ducks a day from a layout boat on the Chesapeake Bay. To the contrary, our method of hunting was walking miles along the likes of Rabon Creek and cutting off the curves. It worked like this.

Either Sammy's granddad, Carlos Boyd, or occasionally my mom or dad, would at midmorning let Sammy and me out on the steel bridge three miles upriver from the sandpit. The rendezvous at dark would be McPherson's Bridge. More out of habit than necessity, as soon as we stepped off the bridge I unplugged my A5 Browning and shoved in five high brass #4s, Blue Peters we called them. The two of us would ease down the creek, slipping along very slowly, single file, watching each step, and paying attention to where we put our boots down. It was vital that we avoid every noisy leaf and not snap a single stick.

The creek was familiar territory. We had made this hunt dozens of times. We knew this river. We knew every sandbar, acorn tree, and every curve. Sometimes we saw the V-shaped wakes of the feed ducks before they sensed our presence or knew we had slipped around them. Other times we just assumed the ducks would feed in an upcoming stretch of water because they had been there many times before.

In any case, on an unspoken command, one of us would stop and take up position by a large tree near the water's edge. The other would cut away from the creek, ease as quietly as a ghost a long way in and around the bend, slip back close to the riverbank, and wait. Now the unsuspecting ducks were between the two of us. At the appropriate time whoever had stayed upriver began his move, slowly pushing the ducks to his partner who was waiting in his ambush position below the curve. As the ducks began to sense danger and the growing threat, they would begin drifting on the current down the river, or at other times they would immediately jump and take flight. Either way, both hunters were likely to get a shot or maybe two, if lucky.

The possible outcomes to this time-tested strategy were as numerous as the hunting trips. Anything could and did happen. The ducks were smart, alert, and unpredictable.

I recall one spectacularly beautiful Saturday in late October when Sammy and I were working Rabon Creek. On one particular curve I stopped and let Sammy go around. I would soon be pushing the ducks. The hunter that went around always had the advantage. He would also have high expectations of a shot because the ducks were normally fleeing the danger they sensed from the hunter pushing them from upriver.

When I stopped by a big red oak about five feet from the creek's edge, Sammy slipped off to the left and down below the sparkling and sunlit curve. I waited, leaning against the tree just in the shadow of its wide trunk. In the woods, if you were still, really still, and you stayed in the shadows, you became almost impossible to see. It was a trick taught by older hunters to us from early boyhood.

Knowing it would take Sammy twenty minutes or more to make a proper cut around, my mind shifted into neutral. I was enjoying the beautiful fall weather and listening to the hypnotic sound of the slow-flowing creek. About ten minutes into my day-dreaming I vaguely became aware of colorful leaves floating downstream on the lazy sunlit current. Big, bright leaves of all colors slowly passed. I snapped out of my trance when I realized that mingled in the leaves were wood ducks. Twenty or more were riding high on the current of the river without moving a muscle. I watched as they basked in the warm sunshine and effortlessly drifted downstream.

Mixed in with the floating sycamore and sweet gum leaves, the brightly colored males were almost perfectly camouflaged in this flotilla of fall color. I finally sorted out what was what and started up with my gun. It seemed the whole creek exploded. I wasted the first shot on a drake so close I could have hit it with a broom. I connected on two and three, missed my fourth shot, and dropped one last male that tried to sneak back upriver. Sammy never shot. He had not yet made it back to the river when the ducks flushed. As I waded back on tiptoes from across the creek, picking up three woodies that fell back in the creek, he stepped to the water's edge, stuck his strong hand out, and helped me up the bank. My numb bare feet complained about the sharp sweet gum balls with every step. As I put on my clothes, I could tell Sammy was disappointed he missed such a big bunch of ducks, but that was hunting. Who would have expected ducks floating by from that part of the river we had already hunted?

Our method of hunting took a bunch of walking. We never shot a lot of ducks on any one day, but we hunted often and hard so it was productive for two young teenage boys. Each trip was a grand adventure. On those glorious, carefree crisp October days with that perfect mixture of fall color and sunshine, what more could there possibly be worth doing?

At times, however, Sammy could not go hunting. Some long put off book report or yard chores would, on occasion, interfere with our plans, requiring me to go alone. At these times I never hunted one of our regular places. Instead I would explore some new part of the creek. There was a section of Rabon Creek that only I had permission to hunt, an arrangement stemming from the friendship between my granddad and the landowner. I protected the privilege by sticking closely to their agreement. One of those days when Sammy was duty-bound to some mundane chore like cleaning out the garage, I talked Mom into dropping me off one bridge higher up Rabon Creek than Sammy and I had ever hunted. Part of this section would fall in the boundary of my special hunting place – a part I had yet to explore.

Mom, always a little more reluctant when I was hunting alone, dropped me off at the upper bridge, making me promise to meet her at the Princeton Bridge right at dark. I could not be late. Promise given, I stepped off the narrow tar-and-gravel road and started the long walk in my hip boots, blue jeans, canvas hunting coat, and favorite hunting cap. The first half of this new stretch was tough going. The creek broke apart and spread out into many little branches, forcing me to cross and recross these tributaries. In places the banks were thick with bushes higher than my head. I heard several ducks fly up ahead of me, spooked by the noise I was making as I pushed through the thick under-growth, but I never saw one. It was just too thick.

About the time I had decided I would have to leave the creek altogether and climb to higher ground if I was to meet my ride on time, the creek worked its way back together. When I came to a substantial five-strand barbed wire fence, I took this to be the upper boundary of the land I had been given permission to hunt.

I found a dry spot, carefully slid my gun under the fence, and rolled under the bottom strand. The land here was sandy. The creek was back within well-defined banks. Huge water oaks grew here, and it was much more open, making this section loaded with possibilities.

Sometimes a creek just feels ducky. There's not a way to really explain it. A hunter just knows when ducks are nearby. As I approached this section of the creek, I got the feeling and slowed down, just barely easing forward.

I glanced up and smiled to myself. The curve ahead – several hundred yards long – was outlined by the gnarly branches and distinctive golden leaves of mature water oaks. Acorns, thick on every limb, were prime duck food! Only thing was, the creek's bank was covered in river cane – waist-high, lush, green, thick, and noisy.

I slowed my pace and eased through this dense growth as best I could. I hadn't gone fifty yards when I picked up telltale V's in the current. Ducks ahead were swimming close to the bank, hidden by the cane. I couldn't see them yet, but they were there. How many was anyone's guess. I slid forward as best as I could, very slowly, carrying my gun in my right hand and parting the cane with my left. I winced at every step, knowing that I sounded like a herd of buffalo. After thirty more yards I caught a glimpse of my quarry. Twenty or so bull mallards, already alerted by the noisy intrusion, had begun swimming away from the bank to the center of the creek – all heads erect, up high as they would stretch. Forty pairs of eyes, some of the best in the business, were locked onto my hunched figure, frozen in mid-stride. Left foot still lifted, I tried to lower my head to shade my face and eased my foot down at the same moment. They were just out of range so the best I could hope for was they would settle down, allowing me to somehow continue my stalk. Nothing doing. They couldn't quite make me out in the thick cane, but they had heard enough. Taking no chances, they exploded as one into the fall sky.

Few things are more beautiful in the hunting world than a flock of ducks, silhouetted against a clear, azure autumn sky. They fought their way expertly through the network of water oak branches, climbed swiftly, and, as usual, circled back over me at a safe two-hundred-foot altitude. Then they disappeared down-river.

As I remembered to breathe, I thought, *That was a very impressive drove of ducks to be this far upriver. A surprise to be sure and a secret worth keeping!*

As I pushed on through the cane, I kept looking over my shoulder to see if I could find any better way to get through this maze without making so much noise. I hadn't gone forty yards when I realized something ahead of me was making more noise than I was. I stopped, a little frightened. Something was coming straight at me, and I couldn't make out what it was. Within minutes I was surrounded by big fat cows, grazing their way through the lush cane, led by a fifteen-hundred pounder, her copper bell tolling the herd along. African elephants would have made less noise.

These were not the prized black cows of Mr. Jack Whitaker, but white-faced Herefords that belonged to Marcus Boyd. I realized then that the fence I had recently crawled under was not the boundary I thought. Now I was on land Mr. Boyd rented to supplement his own pastures. Not moving a muscle, I let the group pass, then continued hunting the beautiful Rabon bottoms to the next bridge without seeing another duck.

Even though I had not fired a shot, I counted the trip a success. I was more than a little pleased. I was in an undeclared race with Sammy to see which one of us could kill forty ducks first.

This newly found group of ducks I could hunt when by myself would help keep me ahead of Sammy and contribute to our two hundred duck goal. Our hunting group, made up of Dad, Big Carlos, Bud, Sammy, Mink, and I, had set our sights on a two-hundred-duck season, something we had never accomplished before. I really wanted to be second high gun. Bud would be number one, no doubt. He was the best shot in our group and in fact, the best shot I ever saw, then or since. But I desperately wanted to be the best of the rest.

During the next couple of weeks I hunted this group of mallards several times, never getting even close enough for a shot.

The ducks were always there in that wide curve, gorging on acorns, completely protected by the thick, noisy cane that warned them of danger.

Then one morning in late November I got a break. As I rolled under the property line barbed wire fence, I could hear the clang and clanking of the lead cow's bell. The herd was again slowly grazing through the cane and coming into the curve.

I thought, *Oh no, the cows will flush the ducks before I even get a chance at them today.*

To make the best of a bad situation, I eased back under the fence and slipped out close to the creek bank. I could just make out the ducks way up in the curve. I knew the cows would spook them, so I got ready for them to flush and maybe, just maybe, I would get a passing shot. The clanging of the bell, growing louder, signaled it wouldn't be very long now. Hearing the steady loud rustling through the cane, I waited. Closer and closer, louder and louder. Clank, clang tolled the bell. I pulled the bill of my camouflage cap down and got my gun ready. It would be but a second or two at the most.

Nothing. Nothing happened.

The entire herd of cows fed through the cane, and the ducks never even lifted their heads for a look-see. I relaxed and knelt down on the sandy bank as the clanging of the bell gradually faded.

I thought, *The ducks are more settled this morning. Today's my day. I'll get a shot.*

I rolled back under the fence, crouched low, and started again through the cane. Even though I was moving as quietly as possible, the ducks took to the safety of the sky before I was twenty yards into the cane. Not getting even a chance at a shot, I was left standing there in the middle of the cane.

It was dead quiet but for the distant noise from the cow's bell. The cow's bell. The clanking of the cowbell! It hit me. It's the noise of the bell! The ducks had become accustomed to the bell and the noise the cows make, but noise in the cane without the sound of the bell puts them on high alert. That's the key!

First thing after school on Monday I walked to Son Duncan's Hardware Store on the square. I can think of nothing that more graphically distinguishes the day in which I now live from my teenage years than the old-fashioned hardware store.

Today's big-box hardware stores carry every nut, bolt, and nail prepackaged in small tightly sealed boxes with plastic windows. You can't buy just the number you need. There's no one there to help you decide what you need. Everything is bar coded, paid for with a credit card, and served up in thin plastic bags. These stores contrast in every way to the locally owned hardware store of the '50s.

Sixty years ago when entering one of these pillars of the town's economy, a bell fastened to the door tinkled announcing a customer's arrival to a friendly, eager, experienced clerk. Quickly meeting his patrons to offer assistance, he would engage them in polite conversation while personally escorting them to the item they wished to purchase. This person most likely knew everyone's name and kinfolk. Back then it was possible to actually touch and examine the items to be bought without gazing through today's impenetrable blister packs. Dark oil floors creaked a little, light came from single naked bulbs hanging from elaborately patterned tin ceilings, and the shelving was all wood-topped with a carved cornice. A rolling ladder facilitated access to the upper level of shelves. If the hardware store did not stock the item desired, it probably was not needed.

I truly miss many aspects of the past.

As soon as I entered the store, Mr. Martin, right there as always, was ready to wait on me. I liked Mr. Martin and his wife. She had been one of my teachers in school and if not for her I might not have passed fifth grade.

I told Mr. Martin I needed to buy a bell. Without hesitation, he turned and asked over his shoulder, "What size you need, Johnny? Cowbell, goat bell, hunting dog bell?"

He quickly produced several sizes and two materials – copper and tin. After Mr. Martin demonstrated the different tones and showed me the prices, I decided on a #4 tin cowbell that cost fifty cents. It sounded the most like the one I had heard up on Rabon Creek.

While Mr. Martin stuffed paper around the clapper, wrapped my purchase in thick brown paper, and tied it with cotton string, I rummaged through a gallon-size Mr. Peanut jar on the counter. Converted to storage for loose shotgun shells, it held all different gauges and shot size and mixed colors. The little white card on the glass jar read:

I was hoping to find several 12-gauge high brass ones, but the demand during duck season had already depleted the supply.

"Anything else I can help you with, Johnny?" Mr. Martin wanted to know.

"No sir, but thanks. I think this will do the trick," I replied.

When I got home I took my new purchase, and my gun and headed off into the backyard to practice. I thought my experiment might make me look a little foolish, and I didn't want my two younger sisters laughing at me.

Needing both hands free to carry, shoot, and reload my gun when stalking the mallard ducks, I determined I needed to put the bell somewhere other than in my hands. I undid my belt, pushed the end through the loop welded to the top of the bell, and refastened my belt. In order to get an accurate feel of how this plan was going to work, I bent over into a crouch, carried my gun at the ready in both hands, and pretended to be slipping through the four-foot-high cane.

No sound. Nothing! The bell didn't make a single respectable clank. It was clear the bell needed more freedom of movement, so I loosened my belt a full two notches and simulated my assault once again. Nothing. Still no sound. A little disappointed with my new idea, I removed the bell altogether and shook it by hand. Sounded great, but now it was clear the bell itself must have a lot of freedom to move if I was to be the great deceiver.

The bell obviously comforted the ducks when hung around the cow's neck, I decided, so I removed my belt, leaving it threaded through the cowbell. I then ran the free end through the buckle to the first hole and re-fastened the belt. The big loose loop with the bell hung freely. I looked around and seeing no one, I slipped the belt over my neck, resumed my crouch position, picked up my gun, and began my make-believe stalk. Though the bell did make a single note clank, it did not have the rhythm of the cow's bell. I tried some different head and shoulder motions and the sound got better, but not by much.

As I kept experimenting I found that if I pushed my hips right and at the same time I threw my shoulder to the left, then quickly repeated the movement, now pushing my hips left and shoulders right, the movement simulated some popular dance step I had seen. I knew I looked ridiculous and would have died

if my buddies had seen me, but I was getting a pretty good imitation of the lead cow. I believed not only the ducks, but even the
cows themselves, might be fooled. I practiced in secret several
more times during the week.

Early Saturday morning I stuffed some paper around the
clapper, jammed the tin bell in the left pocket of my hunting coat,
dropped a handful of shotgun shells in my pocket, and headed to
upper Rabon Creek with Dad. He dropped me off, and I began
my three-quarter-mile walk to the cane patch.

When I reached the barbed wire fence that separated the
lower pasture from the canebreak, I stopped and just listened for
a good five minutes. I did not hear a sound from the cows which
was perfect. Just at the end of my wait I heard, a hundred yards
or so up the big curve, the distinctive four-note call of an old gray
mallard hen.

"Quack, quack, quack, quack."

I smiled to myself, rolled under the bottom strand, checked
that I had five shells in my Browning, and took my belt off. Once
I pulled the cowbell out of my pocket, I removed the paper
around the clapper and threaded the bell onto the belt. After
hanging the loop over and around my neck, I began a slow but
steady stalk through the cane toward Suzy Q. She would lead me
to the big bull green heads.

I did not try to be quiet. The cows were big and noisy as
they forced their wide bodies through the dense cane. I did not
want the ducks to be cautious of someone slipping up on them. It
was vital that they hear, beginning at a distance, the noise of their
non-threatening river neighbors. In a half crouch, gun ready, I
moved forward, elbows spread wide to brush against more cane
and increase the effect of my approach.

Hips swishing back and forth, shoulders swaying right to left, I gave the bell a nice rhythm. After I had gone about seventy-five yards I calculated I was getting pretty close to the ducks. None had spooked yet, and I questioned whether the big drove of mallards was there at all. Had they paddled upriver? Was I now below them? Had they merely floated down current? Was I still too far away? I tried to assure myself that they were where they were supposed to be. I was close, very close.

The anticipation, expectation, and thrill of the hunt had my adrenaline really flowing. The temptation was to slow down, be careful, try to be quiet as possible, but I had seen repeatedly that this had produced an unsuccessful action. I pushed ahead, clanking and clanging, sounding as much like a herd of hungry cows as I could. Another twenty yards more and I began to see water through the cane.

I was almost to the creek bank when the explosion took place. By instinct I raised my gun to my shoulder, remembering to bury my cheek into its cool stock. The sky became a blur of green heads, tan tummies, and orange feet. A whirl of thirty odd pair of wings was fighting for altitude. My trick had almost worked too well. I could have caught some of the surprised ducks with my hands. Most did not even know where I was yet, so some were taking off right over my head. Two crossed just at the touch of the trigger and dropped with my first shot, very unusual. I caught a drake escaping to my left not fifteen yards away and got another clean kill. I missed my third shot but caught a big male working his way through the water oak branches with number four. Marking, in my subconscious, where that one fell, I swung on a hen skimming along just above the top of the cane and really carrying the mail. I got ready to pull the trigger, calculated I was way behind her, pushed the barrel ridiculously far ahead, and she fell like a rock.

Still looking at the commotion all around me, I quickly shoved two more #4s in the receiver and heard the distinct sound of my empty Browning automatic gobbling up more rounds. For a half-second all was quiet as I scanned the creek. A mallard drake, in all his glory and highlighted by a single shaft of sunlight, tried to sneak out. I missed him with the first shot but got the range and speed right on my last chance and dumped him back in the creek.

This last bird was the only one to fall into the water. I hurried downstream far enough so that I could get below him and have time to pull off my boots, pants and underwear. On numb tiptoes I waded to midstream, reached as far out as I could, and dragged him to me with my gun barrel. Those last few steps into deeper icy water can be very interesting. Keeping the water below your hips is a really good idea if you can manage it.

Back on the bank I dried off with my tighty-whities and pulled on my pants. Without any underwear I zipped up very carefully, struggled with pulling thick socks on damp feet, and gladly felt warm boots follow suit. I stuffed my wet underwear in the oversized pocket of my hunting coat and began collecting my ducks.

Just as I started poking through the thick waist-high cane for my last bird, I heard a commotion that stopped me in my tracks. I popped my head up out of the brush and stood very still, listening. Again, the familiar, but unwelcomed, sound shook the normally serene riverside. That long drawn-out bawl only comes from a lovesick bull during mating season. It seemed this two-thousand pound specimen, just like the ducks, had associated the cowbell with the small herd. This big fellow had no intention of delaying a date or being second in line. He was literally racing toward me and destroying a good portion of the riverbottom fauna while looking for love.

I wasted no time in locating my last kill and bending down to snatch up my only hen. The cowbell, which I had completely forgotten, clanged, creating a nice imitation of the real thing and bringing an immediately excited and determined bellow from the would-be dad. I started parting some bushes myself, the bell noisily clanking back and forth with every stride.

I kept repeating in my head, *I've got to get to the property line fence before that big fellow gets any closer.*

The bull and I were in a real footrace, and I was losing. The harder I ran the faster and louder the bell clanged. The bull, it seemed, took this change in position as a playing hard to get tactic by his prospective girlfriend. He became aroused even more by the challenge.

Getting pretty close to the fence line and running as fast as heavy rubber boots, five fat ducks, and a loaded shotgun would allow, I was thinking all the way, *Get to the fence, throw the ducks over, lay the gun on the other side as fast as possible, roll under the bottom strand without getting tangled, pick everything up, and run like hell.*

Sure the bull would stop chasing me when he reached the fence, I still wanted to put as much distance as I could between us. Ten yards from the safety of the barbed wire, I allowed myself a quick glance over my shoulder only to see the bull running full tilt. In the 29° temperature, thick vapor was exploding out of both nostrils. That's all the encouragement I needed.

Bell still clanging with my every move, I hit the fence line and executed my escape plan in lightning speed. On the other side I jumped up hanging onto all my ducks and gear, and tore out of there, still running. Taking a breath and feeling considerably safer, I again stole a look over my shoulder at the exact moment that the bull, at full speed, smashed into the barbed wire. Two cedar posts, one on either side of his massive shoulders, snapped off at ground level as if they were mere matchsticks. Though dragging a tangled mess of wire and broken fenceposts through the woods, nothing in the least impeded the bull's progress.

The raging bull, pulling two partial cedar posts and five strands of barbed wire was all I needed to see. On the fly, it finally dawned on me that I had to get rid of the bell! I pulled the leather belt with its attached bell off my neck and flung it over the first snag I passed, the bell swinging on the bare limb and still clanging as I sped ahead. A hundred yards further down the riverbank, I was exhausted and just had to stop and catch my breath. Looking back, I saw the old rascal, more than a little frustrated. Covered in tangled strands of barbed wire, he was snorting, pawing the ground, tossing his massive head and horns from side to side, and looking everywhere for his coy girlfriend.

Certain that the bull was no longer following me, I quietly walked the mile back up Rabon Creek to the bridge. I was thrilled that my plan had come together and that I had shot well. I figured in a few days the ducks would most likely settle down and return to the curve. I could retrieve my belt and bell and I could try the same trick again, but then was it worth it? That was a lot of bull!

ATLAS SPINNERS

In the late 1950s and early '60s when I was a young boy, if I was not hunting or fishing, one of the most fun things was to go with my dad to Son Duncan's Hardware Store. Folks in our town of 6,000 did not go to town; rather they went to the square. Smack in the middle of a grassy block was an imposing, light-gray stone courthouse surrounded on all four sides by a series of stores and small businesses.

Only three of these establishments I cared a thing about. Belk's department store stocked Boy Scout uniforms and accessories. Poe Drug belonged to my great-uncle and served the best handmade chocolate ice cream sodas. And Son Duncan's Hardware Store sold just about anything else a young boy wanted. A trip to the hardware store with Dad on a cold, rainy day, when there was nothing much else to do, was a great adventure!

I was intrigued with the variety of goods at Son Duncan's. The store sold every kind of tool for gardening; equipment for raising chickens, rabbits, pigs, goats, horses, and cows; carpentry tools and supplies; steel foot traps of all sizes; farming supplies and tractor parts; Coleman lanterns and hand-pumped kerosene fuel; wagon wheels and mule collars; and hunting supplies that included ammunition, rifles, and shotguns. Surprisingly, few hardware stores carried fishing supplies. Son Duncan's had one

127

notable exception: Atlas Spinners, the common code name for dynamite – dynamite, that is, used to catch fish.

In the '50s, dynamite was readily available. Almost every hardware store sold it in all kinds, lengths, sizes, and strengths. Dynamite, sold usually by the fifty-pound case, cost about forty to fifty dollars. You could also buy it by the stick. Popular sizes of dynamite were quietly given a code name. For example, a 1-1/4 inch x 8 inches long stick that had a higher than normal amount of nitroglycerin was called a Farmer's Friend.

A farmer who had some bottomland that stayed too wet for cultivation used this type most often. Needing any standing water to drain into a nearby creek, the farmer could either dig ditches by hand, a time-consuming, labor-intensive job, or he could buy a case of Farmer's Friend dynamite. By placing a stick every two feet across the wet field, he only had to light the first stick. When it exploded, the extra nitroglycerin content would set off the second one, then the third, and so forth, until the whole line of dynamite had exploded in rapid succession. The explosions created a trench and threw dirt out over the field, leaving a nice clean ditch and level field. The entire process took an hour – a real farmer's friend.

Similarly a smaller 1 inch x 6 inches variety manufactured by the Atlas Powder Company had a fuse that would burn under water. It was highly effective for catching large quantities of fish – thus the name Atlas Spinner. Using Atlas Spinners to catch fish was just as effective, and just as illegal, as shooting bull mallards over wholegrain corn. The practice was not altogether unheard of, however.

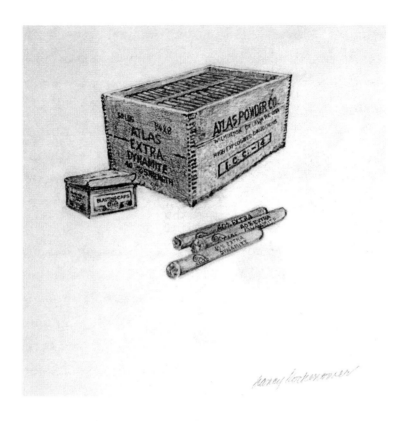

The one fisherman who stood out in my mind when it came to shooting dynamite was Furney Rhem, first cousin to my good friend Esther Johnson. Furney's favorite lure was an Atlas Spinner. I must tell you about the day I met Furney. It began two hours before dawn.

Esther and I had only decided late the previous night to squeeze in an early morning fishing adventure.

We left from her single wide trailer next to Pawleys Pier, drove up US 17 to Litchfield Beach, crossed the small bridge, and took the creek road. When the pavement ended I got out and turned the hubs on the front wheels to engage the four-wheel drive in Esther's faded yellow International Scout. I never figured out the age of this marvel of deteriorating metal. Its wheel well panels were rusted out, and the huge holes in the door on the passenger side allowed a view outside. An inch of beach sand perpetually covered the floors. The car had always looked like it had been, as the saying goes, rode hard and put up wet. I had never seen it any other way.

We followed the headlights as they bore through the predawn sea mist. The ruts and wallows wound through the soft sand all the way to the south end inlet. It was only there we could turn left, pick up the hard-packed sand, and head back north just above the advancing tide.

If anything, the total blackness and piercing headlights actually helped us spot the slough in the rising surf. A sheer two-foot drop-off at the high-water mark and the steeply sloping beach below foretold a deep hole soon to be a perfect fishing spot as the incoming tide persisted over the outlying bar. Esther backed the Scout as close to the high-water mark as we dared and let down the tailgate.

In the darkness the only sounds were the moan of the surf and a soft whine of the wind in the chromed rod guides. With the nine-mile-per-hour breeze from the northeast – it was going to be a good morning. We made our first cast, set the two ten-foot medium weight fiberglass surf rods in the aluminum sand spikes, and for a minute watched the rhythmic up-and-down of the tips. Satisfied the pyramid weights were holding, we pulled out well-used folding lawn chairs and, by the glow of a small flashlight, poured two cups of steaming coffee. We never got to take so much as even one sip.

The first strike practically pulled Esther's rod and sand spike into the ocean. Watching her stubby legs and bare feet churn through the coarse sand almost caused me to miss the growing arch in my own rod.

The bite was on and the pace remained steady right up to dawn.

Bam! Another good strike. A fun few minutes of give-and-take with my sixth fish and he was in the suds.

I waited an extra five seconds, caught a three-foot swell just right, and slid the five-pound spot-tail bass up the steep sandy slope of Litchfield's deserted beach. The sun, struggling to rise above the Atlantic horizon, shot pink and purple rays across a north wind-driven sea. The surf, the color of priceless jade, was so clear I could see right through the curls of the waves. The shafts of first light struck the fish's flanks, turning them the color of polished copper. Two dime-sized ebony spots on its tail gave these handsome fish their name. As I stooped and slid my fingers under its gills, I glanced over to see how Esther was doing. She flashed a big smile and simultaneously set the hook on her own solid strike.

Setting the hook – fighting the frisky, broad-shoulder reds, fumbling with the hooks in the dark – getting the fish back in the water, cutting the finger mullet in two, and then recasting resulted in close to a dozen hookups before the sun brushed pink on the cheek of the eastern sky. Seagulls were diving, and squadrons of pelicans were jabbing through the dawn. The action came faster and faster, but I knew we were on borrowed time. Esther was due at the hunting lodge on the Black River in Rhems, South Carolina, by 11:00 A.M.

As I sliced up a fresh mullet on the tailgate, out of the corner of my eye I saw a small yellow airplane make a banking turn over the inlet between Pawleys Island and Litchfield. It dropped low and headed straight down the beach toward the spot where we were fishing. With fish hitting on every cast, I finished the bait cutting, rigged up, and headed out knee-deep to cast. As I put the rod tip over my right shoulder, the plane crossed over the parked

Scout forcing me to actually duck. I had never seen a plane fly that low before. Esther was laughing at my reaction.

As my two-ounce pyramid sinker hit the water I glanced in the direction of the plane in time to see it bank again sharply and head back toward us. This time the plane was even lower. I worked my fish even while watching as the plane dropped lower and lower, finally landing on the damp sand. The pint-sized plane bounced once on its balloon tires and settled expertly above the breakers. It taxied up to Esther. She had backed out of the surf with her line still in the water and she began to chat with the pilot as he hung out of the open window. When I landed and released my latest fish, I loaded my rod into the holder on the front bumper of the Scout and walked over to meet the guy who dared to land an airplane on this narrow strip of sand with a rapidly rising tide.

As I got closer I heard the pilot say to Esther, "I hear you're chief cook tonight."

"Yeah, got to leave shortly and head to the lodge. Stopping by to pick up the hog and some craft paper over at the paper mill first though," Esther was saying.

As I reached the plane, Esther said, "Hey Billy, want you to meet a friend, Johnny Faris. He goes to Georgia Tech, and he came down for a couple of days of fishing."

"Johnny, this is Billy Davis."

As I stuck out my hand I noticed Billy's left arm had been cut off at the elbow. *Holy cow*, I thought, *a daredevil bush pilot with only one arm! How in the world does he fly this thing?*

"Glad to meet you, Johnny. Catching any fish?" Billy asked.

I slipped a glance over to Esther. Fishermen had strict unwritten rules about answering this type question. One, if you never want the person to fish in your hot spot, you might dodge the question altogether and say, "We're just getting started. Wind's not helping any. We'll just have to see."

Two, if the person is a pretty good friend but not an avid fisherman, the answer might be, "Just a couple. Nothing too impressive."

Third, if he's a good friend who fishes with you and lets you in on where he's found fish running, you might answer, "Burnin' 'em up. Can hardly keep bait in the water. Want to borrow a rod and try?"

The answer to Billy was Esther's call. This was her fishing territory. Her smile back at me was a thumbs up that answer number three was appropriate here. Billy's response was, "Great! Wish I could, but I better get this crate out of here."

Billy stretched out of the window as far as possible and looked back down the beach where he had just landed. We followed his gaze and saw several places where the incoming waves had already erased his tire tracks.

In parting Billy said, "Might see you up at the lodge tomorrow. What time's the big dinner?"

"Fish fry tonight about dark, pig picking's at noon tomorrow," was Esther's reply.

Billy hit the ignition and the prop made a couple of revolutions, coughed, belched white smoke, and caught. He pulled the plane as close to the sand dunes as his right wing would allow, spun it around expertly, and lined her up with the rapidly disappearing hard sand.

Standing on the brakes, he pushed the throttle to the wall, waved once, and shot off down the beach. Every time the plane hit an incoming wave it slowed down as salt water splashed to the bottom of the seaward facing wing. After what seemed way too long, the nose finally lifted and the plane rose into the sky. I watched Esther as her eyes followed the plane's now silent climb. With admiration in her voice she remarked, "That Billy's a piece of work. We better pick up and get going."

Once back at Esther's trailer we washed off the reels, stuck the remaining finger mullet in the fridge, showered, changed clothes, and packed an overnight bag. We would be spending tonight at the hunting lodge on the Black River near Mingo Creek. We switched to my six-cylinder station wagon and headed south down US 17 to the paper mill in Georgetown. We would need to make several stops before driving up Brown's Ferry Road to the lodge in Rhems, the closest place with its name on a map. Our pick-up list included a 120-quart cooler with ice from the fish market on High Street, a sixty-pound pig, its head still on and ready for the grill, a partial roll of wide and heavy craft paper, and a chain saw.

We loaded the cooler with a layer of five inches of ice on the bottom. We stopped at the gatehouse to the International Paper Company and picked up a partial roll of paper the third-shift supervisor had left for Esther. Then we drove to Brown's Meat Market where we tore off a piece of the thick paper and fit it in the cooler to cover the ice. Two men carrying a pig draped in cheesecloth ceremoniously laid it on the paper-covered ice. The last stop was Jenkins Small Engine and Repair Shop where Esther's Homelite chain saw had been sharpened and tuned up. It was ready to go. Into the backseat it went.

All of this preparation was to fulfill a promise Esther had made to the young pastor of All Saints Episcopal Church, who was hosting a three-day fishing/camping/pig cooking weekend for his teenage youth group. Esther, who had donated the pig, was in charge of the fifteen-hour cooking of the hog. Because I just happened to be close at hand, I was designated to be her assistant cook. Since I had never seen a whole hog cooked out-doors, I mostly was the step-and-fetch-it designee.

With all items stowed, I drove up Brown's Ferry Road toward Kingstree.

Esther informed me, "Johnny, the pastor has planned a big fish fry for the teenagers and their families tonight. The teenagers brought their fishing gear this afternoon. Hopefully they will catch enough fish for the cookout. I've been a little worried because of the large crowd coming, so I called my cousin Furney to help out." Esther chuckled, "We won't have anything to worry about with Furney there." Still chuckling, Esther looked at me and added, "Furney's fond of dynamite fishing."

"Are you kidding?" I asked.

"No, I'm not kidding. Furney loves to shoot dynamite. I've never known him to fish without it. In fact, a couple weeks ago, Furney, my cousin Bethel, and my second cousin Sel Hemingway took the big boat Furney sharecrops with Sel's dad, Edsel, from here on the river down to Georgetown, out past the jetties, into the ocean, and all the way to Pawleys Pier. I was working in the restaurant and got this call on the CB radio. 'Mingo Mud calling Pawleys Pier. Come in, Esther.'"

I answered back, "Furney, that you? Where are you?"

"We just off the pier. Come on out here."

Well, I left what I was doing, went all the way out to the very end of the pier, and there, sixty feet below, are Furney, Bethel, and Sel, bobbing up and down in that boat. I yelled down to them, 'What ya'll doing way out here Furney?'"

Furney hollered, "They catching anything up there?"

I looked back down the pier at a line of fishermen on both sides and hollered back to Furney, "They catching a few, not too many."

"What they catching?" Furney wanted to know.

"A few spots, some whiting, a couple of blues, not too much though," I answered.

"Well, we gonna try'em," Furney responded as he pulled the boat back from the pier about fifty yards.

Esther laughed a little. "I knew what was coming, but couldn't stop it. About the time Furney got back a'ways from the pier, he stuck the twelve-inch fuse and the #6 blasting cap into a stick of dynamite, then held the end of the fuse to the end of the stubby cigar he's always smoking. He watched the fuse catch and burn for about five seconds, then casually tossed it overboard. When the blast came, fish by the scores floated to the surface, attracting a tremendous crowd to the pier's railings. Furney, with a long-handle net in his hand, and a big grin on his face, hollered up to me, 'That's your problem, all those folks up there using the wrong bait!'"

Furney added, "Atlas Spinner, best bait ever. Works freshwater, saltwater, anytime, day, or night!"

All the way up Brown Ferry Road Esther looked out her window, laughed, and told story after story about Furney's antics with dynamite. She seemed somewhat preoccupied as if she were looking for something in particular. I was making good time when she announced she had to change clothes. I said, "Let me find a turnout and I'll stop." I started to slow down.

"No, no, keep driving. I can change in the car," she answered as she leaned over the backseat and pulled out a long-sleeve cotton shirt and khaki pants.

"Just turn your head a little, and I'll change," she instructed as she began removing her short-sleeve shirt.

I was doing sixty and she's wanting me to turn my head? I'm thinking, *This is nearly impossible.* I had never seen any women but my mother, on rare occasion, in this state of disrobing. The thought ran through my mind, *Here I am, playing hooky from college. My parents think I'm studying in Atlanta for a big test, but I'm flying down a long, backwoods road with a nearly naked woman. Lord, please don't let me have a wreck! Please!*

Once fully clothed again and a little further up the road as we approached a clear-cut, Esther directed, "Turn in the next pull-out."

I slowed, turned into the next sandy logging road, and noticed Esther was carefully studying something out her open window. Finally she announced, "This will do." I cut off the engine and we got out.

Once we folded the rear seat down and pushed the cooler up against the front seat, we had a good bit of space for I knew not what, but soon learned. Esther grabbed her chain saw and started out across the thick brush. I knew now why she had changed out of her short pants and short-sleeve shirt. I was very glad that I just happened to be wearing long pants, good boots, and long sleeves.

We passed several young, straight trees but only stopped when we were in front of a good-for-nothing, stubby, twisted, twelve-foot specimen. Esther looked up and down that tree, evaluating its worth. With a little gleam in her eye and a reverent voice, she announced, "Blackjack Oak. I don't cook with nothin' else." Starting the saw with one impressive motion, she cut the tree off at the ground. In twenty minutes she had de-limbed it and blocked it into twelve-inch logs, and I had hauled and loaded every scrap neatly into the back of the wagon.

Ten minutes up the road we turned onto the sandy road leading to the lodge overlooking Black River. Once alongside the screen door, we each grabbed our small overnight bags and entered. A large, open room, paneled in cypress and floored in wide heart pine boards, had that welcoming, cozy feel. The young pastor and his wife were already here and had settled into one of the three bedrooms on the back of the lodge. Esther and I each chose one of the two remaining. Tossing our bags on the bed, we were out the door again. Knowing we had much to do, Esther was all business.

Conveniently, the fire pit, constructed of two layers of 12-inch concrete blocks, was just a few yards to the right of the lodge as was a modified 55-gallon oil drum. The deeply charred drum, with its bottom cut out, was sitting on a coarse grate held in place with four concrete blocks. This, I was to learn, was a piece of equipment very essential to the success of a pig cooking.

Esther directed me to move the station wagon up near the drum and stack off the blackjack oak. Right away she built a fire – a really big fire – in the drum. Flames were shooting out the top in no time. We spread another long piece of the craft paper out on a substantial picnic table and laid out the pig on this clean work surface. Esther washed the whole thing with a damp cloth and spent a good forty minutes doing whatever you do to a pig before putting it on to cook.

When she finished this ritual, Esther tore off another sizable piece of craft paper, covered the pig, and turned her attention to the pit. Producing a rake and shovel, both with scorched handles, she asked me to pull out the old ashes. Next I learned the usefulness of the fire drum. As the blackjack oak burned, it formed chunky, angular coals that individually dropped to the ground through the grate. As soon as the ground below the barrel was covered in these coals, I added another log of oak in the top of the barrel to insure a steady, continuous supply of coals.

Esther demonstrated how to shovel these coals out and sprinkle them sparingly over the entire bottom of the pit. Once done, we placed a heavy, iron grill the size of a large screen door over the pit. The lathered-up pig was placed on the grill. Then to my surprise, Esther covered the whole pit, pig and all, with another big sheet of craft paper.

By carefully controlling the supply of hot coals, Esther kept the fire cool enough through the twelve hours of cooking that the paper never scorched. I was impressed with her knowledge of this whole process.

During all this preparation and cooking of the hog, the forty some-odd teens, only a year or two younger than I, had pitched their tents in the yard around the lodge and gone to the river to fish for supper.

After checking on the fire to make sure it suited her, Esther convinced the young pastor to tend the pig cooking for a short time. She and I went down to the river to check on how the fishing was going and to see if Furney had showed up.

Teenagers were scattered out all up and down the better part of two hundred yards along the bank of Black River. Each one had brought his or her own gear and bait creating a Duke's mixture of cane poles, casting rods, and close-faced Zebco outfits. As you would expect, the expertise of these young folks ranged from one end of the spectrum to the other. The task of feeding fresh fried fish to a big crowd that very night was daunting.

I now understood why Esther had thought additional help might be needed, and why she had called in reinforcements. A minute or so later a bright orange boat roared around the bend in the river. It banked sharply in the glass-smooth, dark river water and headed toward the shore where Esther and I were waiting. I judged the boat to be going way too fast, but the man at the boat's console – with the stub of a cigar clenched in the side of his mouth and a straw Panama hat covering his head – cut the 40hp engine at precisely the right moment and coasted to a gentle stop just as the bow touched the bank.

"What'cha doin', Esther?" were the first words I heard Furney Rhem speak.

Esther chuckled, "Trying to come up with enough fish and loaves to feed the five thousand. Thanks for coming."

"Glad to hep out," Furney said as he glanced up and down the bank at some four dozen fully engaged teenagers trying to catch supper.

Furney asked Esther, "How many you 'spectin' tonight?"

"I figure about 150 total," was Esther's reply.

"Good thing you called. I think you may need some hep on the fish. Hop in and let's get to fishing," said Furney.

"By the way Furney, this is my friend Johnny. He's down from Georgia Tech for a few days. We've been fishing the beach."

"Well, Johnny, hop on board. We can use an extra hand."

Furney expertly backed out into the middle of the river and shifted to forward before shooting off upriver like a bat out of hell. It was immediately obvious the boat was rigged with a motor twice the horsepower it was designed for. About a half-mile upriver, Furney pulled the throttle back. We coasted to a stop. Furney stood up from behind the console and looked at one deserted bank, then the other. He looked upriver, then down. At that, he reached into a wooden box under the console and pulled out a short stick of dynamite that had a red waxy look. I was paying very close attention. Although I had seen dynamite bought at the hardware store at home before, this was the first time I was actually seeing it in action. Furney stuffed a blasting cap – its foot-long fuse attached – down into one end of the six-inch stick. He puffed on his short cigar a couple of times to draw an orange glow.

My first thought was, *he's going to light his nose on fire.*

Instead he stuck the fuse to the stogie. Then he pulled the burning fuse to arm's length for what seemed forever and studied it as if it was the first time he had ever seen such a thing.

When he flipped it over the back of the boat, I realized I had been holding my breath for a very long time. The dynamite immediately sank into the dark tea-colored water, but for a brief few seconds I could see the lit fuse disappearing. I silently counted, *"One thousand one, one thousand two, one thousand ...*

The river, as if in slow motion, began forming a big bulge right before my eyes. Like a giant mushroom the bulge grew and grew. The tail end of the boat began to lift, and I instinctively – but uselessly – covered my ears with my hands. When the mushroom could grow no more, it exploded, creating a sound that caught me off guard. Water went everywhere. As the towering water found its way back into the river, a substantial number of freshwater fish floated to the surface in various stages of unconsciousness. To my surprise, they did not appear to be injured – just stunned. Furney handed me a long-handled crabbing net, and showed me how to scoop up the casualties as he eased the boat in, around, and through the flopping fish. I began loading the bright bass, called trout by Furney, and red-breasted bream into the straw basket Esther held.

Once the fish were collected and loaded in the basket, Furney ran further up Black River toward Mingo Creek. There we fished a second time.

In a sharp bend in the river, Furney slowed the boat to just above idle, stood up, and began first looking at the left bank, then the right, and again back left. It was obvious he was using objects on land to triangulate some particular spot on the river, maybe a deep hole. Very shortly he must have nailed down exactly where he wanted to be, because he put the engine into idle and began rummaging in the wooden crate under the steering console for fuses, blasting caps, and a fresh Atlas Spinner.

I glanced over at Esther. She just smiled and chuckled. I thought I'd be ready this time. I put the net where I could quickly reach it, sat down next to Esther on the foredeck for better stability, and again put both hands over my ears. I wasn't ready for what came next.

Furney lit the fuse but lost hold of the stick of dynamite and it fell into the water right beside the boat! Furney reacted by pushing the throttle all the way forward. The only problem was, that flooded the engine and it stalled. We sat dead in the water right over a stick of dynamite that was lit! Furney quickly abandoned his position in the middle of the boat and scuttled to the front of the boat where Esther and I had already gotten ourselves as far forward as we could possibly go. When Furney joined us, the shift in weight brought the back of the boat clear out of the water. Just before all three of us slid off the bow, the dynamite exploded. A very large bulge in the river pushed the bow up and up until the expanding bubble finally burst in a deafening explosion. Water shot twenty feet into the air, lifting the boat and throwing the three of us onto the floor. As the water began to shower back down, a sizable number of fish actually fell into the boat along with a good portion of Black River. As soon as it was clear no one was hurt, the whole episode became hilariously funny and we three got to laughing uncontrollably. I managed to grab the net that had fallen overboard and began dipping up the remaining stunned fish. Furney got the engine going. Esther found a bucket and started bailing out water and putting fish into a second basket.

With two baskets nearly full of fish, we sped back to the lodge's dock. As Furney began easing the boat toward the bank, we noticed a middle-aged man dressed in forest green pants and a khaki long-sleeve shirt. A bright gold shield pinned above his left shirt pocket identified him, obviously, as the game warden.

I began to divorce myself from the net I had been holding and slowly moved to the opposite side of the boat. As it touched the bank, Esther tossed a rope to the fellow and said, "Pull us up a little, Clyde, while we hand these fish over." Esther swung herself over the bow where she had been sitting and motioned for me to hand her the baskets, each containing at least forty or fifty pounds of assorted fish.

Seeing me struggle as I hoisted them to the boat's gunwale, the man in the uniform said, "Here, let me help you." He took the baskets, one at a time, and handed them off to Esther.

I didn't know what was going to happen next. We were obviously breaking the law. If truth be known, probably several laws. Heaven only knew what the limit was. Would this warden write us a ticket, charge us a fine, arrest us, or all three? I kept glancing over to Esther for some indication of what she thought was coming next when she calmly asked, "Clyde, you and Jenny coming tonight, aren't you?"

"Sure," Clyde answered. "Soon as I go by the house and change, I'll be back to help clean fish. Jenny's coming a little later to help."

Clyde turned to go and then turned back. The question I was dreading came. "Furney, looks like you had good luck. What kind of bait were you using?"

Without the slightest hesitation, Furney answered with pride in his voice, "Atlas Spinners."

A MULE EATING BRIARS

The year was 1968. I was twenty-three years old, single, and a brand-new air traffic controller in the United States Navy. Now stationed in Brunswick, Georgia, I was more than a little homesick and looking for something to do with my ample off-duty time.

Having a love of the outdoors and a passion for fishing, I turned my attention to scouting for productive fishing spots in one of the largest and most pristine salt marshes on the east coast. The area, referred to as the Golden Isles of Georgia in the Chamber of Commerce ads, covered approximately 130 square miles and stretched from Cumberland Island National Seashore in the south to Blackbeard Island National Wildlife Refuge in the north.

Not long into my search it was clear I was situated in the middle of an exceptionally productive fishery. I was delighted to begin my spare time hunt south of Brunswick, below Jekyll Island. As I worked my way north on Highway 17, I would drive down any sandy road that led toward salt water.

My methodical search began at the numerous bait shops, tackle stores, and boat landings that dotted the barrier islands along the eastern side of old US 17. Over the years I had observed that these types of places would be decorated with many photographs, some recent and some ancient and tattered, depicting impressive catches of local fish. Every fisherman loves bragging rights, and these local waterfront establishments encouraged their customers to post pictures of successful fishing trips.

These fisherman hangouts all posted photographs curling along the edges with the effects of age and humidity. Fishermen in warm clothes and knee boots were captured lifting heavy strings of washtub-size flounder and impossibly fat winter trout. Sunburned faces beaming at all manner of blue water species hung on display boards boasting the successful boat's name. But it was a small group of 5 x 7 fairly recent black-and-white glossies – tacked way back on a side wall at Two-Way Fish Camp way up in Darien, Georgia, that really grabbed my attention.

The half-dozen pictures, all with different dates, were taken in the early morning, judging by the direction of the sun and sharp shadows. Each photograph showed two men, possibly father and grown son, bracketing ten to twenty large channel bass, sometimes called red fish or spot tail bass. My guess was that these men were locals, a guess confirmed when I began asking around about where the men had caught these fish. I couldn't blame anyone I asked for being noncommittal with fish like that; secrets are guarded closely with polite, but vague, answers. I had responded the same way many times myself when asked where I had caught a particularly nice string of fish. I understood and was neither offended nor discouraged. As the old-timers would always say, "If you're in a hurry, don't fish."

My posting at Glynco Naval Air Station was for three years. I was not going anywhere soon, so I actually looked forward to the challenge of finding the best locations, especially the place where the fish in the photos were caught. One thing was for sure; I would need a boat, a good-sized boat, and it would need to be fast. There was a large area to cover. In addition, I would eventually need to acquire local knowledge of this vast estuary.

During my first spring in coastal Georgia, daylight saving time began, and long afternoons kicked in. After work I began hanging around several of the fish camps and marinas to the north of Brunswick, listening to fishermen chat as they came and went. I offered to help folks back their boat trailer under the lifts, or carry a heavy ice chest to their pickup, hoping to glean information. My goal, in general, was to melt into the local scene and learn every tidbit I could.

The following summer I was granted a thirty-day leave in order to get married. On June 21, 1969, the summer solstice, Claudia Tinsley became my wife. As I write, we have just celebrated being newlyweds for forty-six years.

As you might expect, it was no accident that Claudia was a fisherman, and a good one. Shortly after our honeymoon on Sea Island, we moved into a small two-bedroom apartment on the East Beach, Saint Simons Island.

Not long thereafter we began building a twenty-one-foot center console sport fishing boat – in our living room! All of these promising local hangouts required a relatively shallow-draft boat that could traverse the numerous inlets and breaking surf with a degree of safety. For several years I had been collecting pictures and articles about different types of wooden fishing boats. One night, I showed Claudia an article about a Seattle Dory. These boats were designed by commercial salmon fishermen to be launched off the beach right through the big surf and to negotiate the rough seas of the Pacific Coast. We both thought this style would be a perfect long-term boat for the two of us and the family we hoped to have.

Using a picture in *Outdoor Life* magazine as a guide, I began to draw a set of plans. The boat's flat bottom would curve up sharply in the bow, allowing it to pass through breaking waves. Its sloped transom would deal nicely with a following sea.

The boat's most unique attribute, however, was a motor well. An outboard motor could be mounted completely inside and to the rear of the boat. This type of construction let the propeller to be raised above the bottom of the boat but still move the boat along nicely when the water became skinny. The shallow feature would allow the boat to cross the notorious sandbars guarding the inlets between the barrier islands we would fish. We were sold! This would be our new boat!

By late summer we had turned the living room of our island apartment into a busy woodworking shop. For the framing I had ordered a special type of strong wood from White Plains, New York. Claudia helped cut and glue up each of the wide white oak frames. As soon as one frame was complete, we loaded it into the trunk of our 1967 Chevrolet, tied the trunk lid down, and took it to the site of our childhood homes in Laurens, South Carolina, a trip that was 260 miles each way.

Once all the major structural pieces were completed and delivered to my parents' house, my dad and I erected in the back-yard the jig on which the boat would be assembled. We built the hull upside down on this jig.

Next we constructed a protective shed and covered the entire structure with heavy-duty plastic that would last at least a year, the estimated time frame of construction. The backyard looked as if we had erected a big greenhouse.

Since Claudia and I were from the same hometown, the weekly trips worked out well. She and I would leave right after work on Fridays and drive home with a load of boat parts. Dad

and I worked all day on Saturdays and a few hours after church on Sundays while Claudia visited her family.

One Sunday afternoon when the boat was pretty far along, we hired a wrecker to lift the hull. We turned the boat over, set it on its new trailer, and began the finishing work on the inside. The boat had a nice center console. While dad was busy countersinking #10 2-inch Monel screws in the sides, I was measuring for a seat to stretch across the eight-foot beam width. Claudia stood on a six-foot ladder, watching us work. I pulled the tape measure to 24 inches thinking that width would be an adequate size and looked up at Claudia for approval. She glanced to see if Dad was looking. Seeing he was busy, she cocked up one eyebrow. I thought for a split second and pulled the tape to a more comfortable 40 inches. Her beautiful smile of anticipation raised my heart rate.

149

I thought, *This girl and I are going to have a great summer – just fishing of course!*

Forty-eight weekends and 25,000 miles later, our boat was ready. One sun-drenched warm Saturday Claudia, Dad, and I trailered the boat to nearby Greenwood Lake and slid the *CeeTee* (for Claudia Tinsley) off its heavy-duty galvanized trailer into the water for its maiden voyage.

Our twenty-one foot vessel looked gigantic in the lake where small aluminum johnboats were more common. That morning as *CeeTee* turned more than a few heads of the early spring bass fishermen, we were so pleased with ourselves. The boat did not leak a drop, it was fast, and it handled extremely well. We thought it looked great!

Just building the *CeeTee* was a wonderful time for my dad, my new wife, and me. Those weekends were some of the most enjoyable times we ever had together. Now we were equipped to have some fun locating and catching fish.

The entire year we were building the boat in Laurens, Claudia and I kept knocking around the landings and marinas along Georgia's Highway 17 as time permitted. We met several watermen who made their living crabbing and shrimping. These were not the big operators out of Darien, but local old-timers. We got to know their schedules pretty good and began meeting them at the docks to purchase the makings of a fresh shrimp mull or frogmore stew or some steamed blue crabs.

Once we brought the *CeeTee* to Brunswick and started exploring the seemingly limitless creeks and channels, getting to know these local watermen was even easier. I believe they had a real appreciation for this new no-nonsense craft. They could identify with its look of a real workhorse.

Our boat allowed us to catch these locals out on their regular routes, pull up alongside their vessel, visit a few minutes, and buy some good size bait mullet – still kicking – and our regular dozen crabs or several pounds of shrimp.

One Sunday, very early in the morning, Claudia and I were bringing the *CeeTee* in from an all-night trip. We saw a local we had met before, Proverb Hair, sorting his first drag of the day for creek shrimp. Thinking that fresh shrimp salad sounded like the perfect supper, we slowed. Proverb's homemade thirty-foot trawling net was perfect for these shallow creeks. Its pint-sized wooden spreader boards were equipped with galvanized chains and heavy towropes. The net was an exact miniature of the ones hanging from the outriggers of the commercial shrimp boats.

The effectiveness of Proverb's little rig and his lifetime of experience in these waters was evident. Twenty-odd pounds of number 16/20-count brown shrimp kicking on the sorting board was proof enough for anyone.

"Morning, Pro. Looks like the browns are still in. Nice lookin' catch. Could you spare a couple pounds?" I asked.

"Sure thing. Pass your bucket over. Shoor you only want two?"

I looked over at Claudia and she, thinking like I was of how hungry we already were after an active night out on the water, held up three fingers.

"Better make it three, Pro," I smiled.

He chuckled, his belly jiggling inside his faded denim bib overalls. It wasn't the first time he had successfully traded me up.

His tin scoop, made from a one-pound coffee can, slipped three pounds of glistening translucent green and brown bodies into our bait bucket. We had placed the cash money, as usual, in the bottom of the bucket before we passed it over.

"Where's you been all night?" Proverb casually inquired as he continued sorting the shrimp from the bycatch as it's called by the watermen.

By now, Claudia and I had learned a few of the local names for some of the creeks and islands. We told him we had been try-ing for big channel bass off Rabbit Island.

Casually Proverb inquired, "Have much luck?"

"No," I confessed, "it was a beautiful night but no luck on the big ones. Just a couple puppy drum. We just haven't found the big ones yet. Still looking though."

Without even looking up, Proverb offered, "You's might oughts to try right at the mouth of the Altamaha."

"Thanks, Pro. We'll give it a try on our next trip out. Have a good day and thanks again. See you next time."

As I slowly eased the big boat away, I suspected Proverb had just given us a key piece of information – maybe not a key to the whole puzzle, but a good solid chunk of one corner. I smiled to myself as I pushed the throttle three-quarters open and felt the powerful Evinrude bring us up on plane. The river was still smooth as a mirror at that hour in the morning. Thin patches of fog hovered here and there. The harsh early light on the gold and green marsh grass and the soft swish of the dark water as we slipped through lazy curves signaled the day's beginning following a beautiful night on the water. In the years we were allowed to call this area home, we never grew tired of it.

After receiving Proverb's advice, I couldn't wait to reach our apartment and study my Intracoastal charts that covered that section of the Altamaha River. Two-Way Fish Camp was on the Altamaha River where I had seen, almost a year earlier, the photographs of the big catches of bass. I felt that we were about to find the next piece of the puzzle.

After our six-mile run down the Intracoastal, we unloaded and scrubbed down the boat, arriving at our small, cozy apartment on Saint Simon's Island by 10:00 A.M. We had dozed on the boat through the six hours of incoming and outgoing tide, but we were plenty sleepy as we slipped our supper of shrimp into the fridge. Claudia and I had only been married ten months but had already begun to form that code talk all couples have.

After a night of salt air and summer breezes, the code that seemed appropriate as my wife stepped into the warm shower and looked over her bare shoulder at me was, "We shouldn't waste water." After the first year of being married I fully expected to receive some sort of commendation from the Brunswick Water and Sewer Department for the "most improved in water conservation."

We slept like the dead until five that afternoon when hunger drove us to our galley kitchen. Spreading sheets of yesterday's news we poured out the ice-cold shrimp and started de-heading supper as fast as possible. Claudia heated the water in a heavy aluminum pot and added a handful of salt. By the time the water was roiling, I had cleaned, shelled, and deveined those beauties. Into the water they went. Our simple recipe was once they turned pink, we boiled them just sixty seconds and then into a bowl of crushed ice they went. Once the shrimp were ice-cold, Claudia started on the shrimp salad while the other pound and a half – coated generously with Heinz chili sauce – disappeared as appetizers.

After supper I spread out the navigation chart that covered the mouth of the Altamaha River all the way south along the Intracoastal and below to Troop Creek Marina. We had been trailering the *Cee-Tee* from our apartment up Highway 17 the fifteen miles to Two-Way Fish Camp for several months. Now, however, a small marina had opened at Troop Creek, only two miles from the Naval base and thirteen miles closer than Two-Way. An older couple, Bill and Nancy, had just retired from the Navy. They built the little marina themselves in a convenient location. A super-sized off-road fork truck complimented their newly racked, covered boat storage. Their introductory $25 a month offer included putting the boat in the water and putting back into storage when we returned. Most importantly it fit our $125 per month Navy pay and Claudia's teaching salary. We moved *CeeTee* there the first month the marina opened and parked the heavy galvanized trailer for the duration of our tour of duty.

Now that I thought the mouth of the river would be our target, I roughly calculated it to be an eleven-mile run from Troop Creek to our new fishing spot. Even though the boat run would be longer, not having to trailer the boat up busy Highway 17 would save a lot of time. Bill and Nancy's service of unloading and fueling the boat with just a phone call cut off a total of forty minutes from our old travel time.

Our series of after work fishing/exploring adventures began. On our first trip out of the new marina I missed a turn and went two miles up a dead-end creek. By the time we returned to the main channel and reached the mouth of the big river, it was getting pretty dark. The river was actually wider and rougher than I had expected. I dropped anchor well inside the chop at the mouth, fished two hours, and eased back home when it got uncomfortably rough.

The following Friday night, we left the dock at 6:00 P.M. and arrived at the Altamaha mouth well before dark.

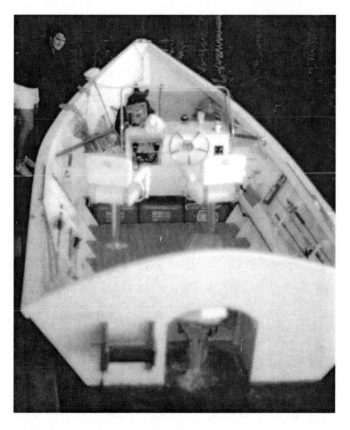

No other boats were anywhere in sight. The water was very calm. Feeling a little more comfortable, I ran closer to the ocean before anchoring in the middle of the river mouth. Claudia and I rigged up the heavy rods with fresh mullet and ate our summer supper. After our picnic, dusk melted into a starlit canopy and the two of us were honeymoon happy. Watching my beautiful wife curl up on the cushioned front seat, feeling the warm breezes and the gentle rocking of the boat were just too much. I set the drags on all four rods and prayed to God that no fish would take the bait this night.

At the first pulse of dawn we reeled up, put the rods in their racks, and ran to the dock by the red and green beacons of the Intracoastal.

Our next trip out was in April – two days before the full moon. We knew the tide would be flood full at 8:30 P.M. and running hard. After leaving the dock, we sped down Troop Creek and hit the Intracoastal before seven o'clock.

About a quarter mile from the mouth of the Altamaha, I could see a boat, good size open job with a big outboard, already ahead of us, the first we had ever seen there. By the look of it, two men were anchoring the boat. It was so far off to the right side of the river, I thought at first they were going to fish the bank. As I drew closer I could see they were actually about fifty yards from the bank and were fishing on the river side. Claudia and I pulled up about mid-river. We dropped anchor about one hundred yards behind them and baited up in about thirty feet of water.

The night was absolutely perfect with its soft breeze, warm temperatures, and moon that was almost full. At dusk Claudia got a good strike. When she tried to set the hook a little too quickly for big spot tails, she missed him. I almost immediately got a hit, waited a few extra seconds, and hit the fish hard. Thirty minutes later I pulled a four-foot shark alongside. You can be sure I cut the thirty pound monofilament leader well ahead of those razor-sharp teeth. As the sun dropped beneath the ocean's horizon, I noticed both men in our neighboring boat were working fish.

While re-baiting our hooks, I wondered if this trip would be another night of just feeding the local trash-fish fresh mullet fillets for six hours. At that moment Claudia's line began to move at a slow, steady pace. The spool on her conventional Penn reel was out of gear and began to turn at a slow, steady pace. The clicker on her reel began to pick up a little. Like a veteran, Claudia was patient this time.

Unable to stand it any longer, I said, "Better hit him."

When Claudia threw the Penn into gear and put a lot of muscle into the set, neither of us had any doubt in our minds that she was into a good fish. Praying she had not hooked a shark, I retrieved the big six-volt Coleman electric lantern out of the console's cabinet and pulled the five-foot stainless steel gaff out of its spring-loaded holder on the transom.

Our eyes had adjusted to the darkness pretty well, and the rising moon provided enough light to play the fish, so I left the light off for now.

The rising tide, running hard, gave all of the advantage to the fish. Claudia was patient though, keeping the pressure on. When her line got within ten feet of the boat, I couldn't wait any longer to catch a glimpse of her fish, one she had been battling for the last fifteen minutes. I flipped the switch on the Coleman and tried to peer through the dark Altamaha water.

The fish did not fight like a ray or shark, but we could see nothing except the leader disappearing into the cone of light that cut through the water only a foot or so. The fish, however, must have seen the light. Twenty yards of line melted from the spool in short order, but the drag worked smoothly, doing its job and allowing Claudia to pump the fish back into the light. This time we caught sight of a wide bronze back glistening in the harsh light.

Our first big bass was just holding in the stiff current when I carefully slipped the gaff through its gills. Claudia and I were ecstatic. Our first truly big red! With some effort, I slid the fish over the gunwales, laid it flopping on the wide planks of the floor, and slipped the hook out of its pulsating jaw. Claudia wound up the slack line and put her rod in the rod holder as I fumbled to open the tackle box and rummaged around for the tape measure.

When I finally found it, she held the light, trembling a little with the adrenaline rush, while I stretched the tape from the tip of its tail to its nose. Thirty-eight and one- half inches! What a handsome and powerful fish it was. We admired its deep-white belly and the three dime-size black spots on its wide, nearly-transparent bronze tail. After taking a quick photo with the Kodak, I said, "Honey, we better get him back in the water. You ready?"

She answered "Yes, he's too pretty to keep. Let's put him back."

I slipped one hand under his head, putting my thumb in one gill and forefinger in the other. Then I placed my left hand around the thinnest part of its warm body near his tail. The heft of our prize felt good as I leaned far out over the high gunwale and held the fish a few seconds in the warm water so that the current forced water through its gills. He quickly sensed freedom, pushed once with that powerful tail, and was gone.

I gave Claudia a big fishy hug. "Great job! I think we've finally found what we've been looking for."

Though we fished two hours of the falling tide, we had little luck. Close to midnight we each poured ourselves a cup of strong coffee steaming from the thermos, pulled anchor, and sped past alternating green and red navigation lights. The coffee was hot, the salt air was in our hair, and we had big smiles on both our faces. Thus began a spring and summer of increasing successes.

In the following weeks I began to piece the pattern together. We seemed to catch more and bigger bass near or on a full moon, when the tide time was half full, and about three hours before darkness. I also noticed the other boat most often on those nights too. I continued to be puzzled, however, why that boat always anchored so close to the marsh in the same location.

We loved the outings together during the fall months, but we weren't quite there yet. Those photographs on the walls of bait shops still set a goal for us. I wanted to prove I could find and catch those big spot tail bass, too. Over the winter we fished trout on the shell banks with live shrimp and enjoyed plenty of great fresh fillets.

One night I spread out the Altamaha chart and located creeks we had not yet explored. My eye naturally looked longingly at that section of map covering our bass spot. Then the solution hit me. The missing piece of the puzzle was right there, but I had not noticed it. Claudia and I had been fishing the center of the river where the channel ran approximately thirty feet deep. It was a location we expected these big bass to feed. However, right next to the marsh on the right side of the river was a sixty- foot hole, one about fifty yards long and forty yards wide. Of course! These old local boys always fished right off our starboard bow close to the marsh above that very pronounced hole. Claudia and I decided that spot would be the first place we would try come next spring.

In early April, Troop Creek Marina decided that sponsoring a bass contest would be good for business. We signed up right away, paid our $25 entry fee, and looked forward to the new season and a little competition. The dates for the full moon in that month didn't quite mesh with our work schedule, but we managed to catch an evening close to the right combination. Once at the mouth of the river, we were somewhat surprised that the other two locals were nowhere in sight. We took this opportunity to pinpoint the hole. After several attempts, we finally found a spot where we could anchor up from the dropoff and then pay out enough rope to fall back where our bait would drift right into the deepest part. Though we did not get a strike that night, we carefully marked the spot by triangulating from the two airship hangars on base – the largest wooden structures in the world – and an ancient cedar tree on shore. We vowed to be back, and back we came. By summer's end we had caught numerous beauties, releasing them all. Trophy fish was our goal so we kept after them. The payoff came on a beautiful late summer night in August. The moon rose out of the Atlantic two days shy of full. The breeze out of the west was just enough to keep the no-see-ums and mosquitoes at home. The water temperature was 72 degrees - perfect bass conditions. As the anchor rope came taught over our hole, Claudia free-spooled a fresh mullet fillet back into the hard running tide. The bass did not disappoint that night. I did not even get my rod out of the holder until Claudia had whispered, "He's on."

"Let him run another ten yards and hit him," I whispered back. Never taking my eyes off her line I started baiting up my own hook. Zzurr —- zzurr – zzzzurrrrrr. Before I could even get my line in the water, Claudia threw the big Penn reel in gear and leaned back hard. The bite was on! Two frantic hours and eight fish later, Claudia had a forty-three-inch keeper. Mine looked to be a twin, but when he hit the scales he was short by two pounds. These two trophies, however, awarded Claudia and me first and third places in that summer's bass tournament.

After we caught those two beauties, we stopped by Proverb Hair's boat next morning and showed him our two prize-winning fish. We thanked him for helping us in those early days. Obviously very pleased with himself, his broad smile showing a mouthful of gleaming white teeth, he truly resembled a mule eating briars!

THE $10,000 TARPON

From early 1969 to the middle of 1971 I found myself in many new and different situations. I graduated from Georgia Tech in January, joined the Navy in February, moved to Saint Simon's Island, Georgia, in March, married in June, started building a twenty-foot boat in August 1969, completed it in May of 1970, and fished some of the most beautiful and productive salt water in the world. Then I was transferred to Guantánamo Bay, Cuba.

The one constant during these months was my long-term friendship with Esther Johnson, who I first met in my early teens. By any measure, Esther was a real tomboy. Short, stocky, and very athletic, Esther was the catcher on the boys' baseball team at her high school. She caught in off-season for her uncle, Flint Rhem, who was pitcher for the St. Louis Cardinals in their 1928, 1931, and 1934 World Series wins. A hunting and fishing guide, Esther could cast a 10-foot surf rod better than most men, and I have seen her triple on a covey rise more than once. Through my teens, Dad and I had the privilege of spending many a crisp fall day chasing spot tail bass and bluefish up and down the deserted South Carolina beaches of Litchfield and Pawleys Island with her.

Esther, as much as anyone, was the reason I finally graduated from college. I hated college. I did not put nearly as much effort

163

into my work there as I could have, and I often had periods when I felt burned out and ready to do something else. It was during these times that I would call Esther and ask if I could come fishing with her. I think she could sense the urgency. She never put me off. She never said no.

Throwing some fishing gear in my car, I would inform my roommate Warren, a straight-A student, of my planned absence and take off for Pawleys Island. Warren was the most talented liar I have ever known. Any phone call that came from Mom to our room during my trips to Esther's were met with a long, elaborate explanation. He created a tale of how busy I was doing research in the library for an extremely important paper and I was all but sleeping in the stacks as I dedicated myself to this week-long task.

Warren was an absolute gem!

For those four years, Esther kept me going. I frequently arrived discouraged and tired at her mobile home, which was perched atop a sand dune right on the beach. The two of us fished hard and ate fresh seafood we cooked ourselves. I would sleep like the dead in between. Then I returned to Atlanta with many an encouraging word from my fishing partner and renewed energy. I owed Esther. She saved my sanity.

Soon after Claudia and I were married and the two of us finished building our boat, we decided to invite Esther to join us on Saint Simons Island for a week of tarpon fishing. I promised to give her a call when the big fish started running, and she agreed to drop whatever she was doing when the call came.

Claudia and I brought our new boat, the *CeeTee*, down from Laurens, South Carolina, where we had built her, to Saint Simons Island. It took us most of June and early July to learn that late summer and early September is great tarpon fishing time in the rivers and sprawling estuaries of the Golden Isles of Georgia. Two-Way Fish Camp, located just off US 17, was the center of this activity. Two-Way was located where US 17 crosses the Altamaha River. We normally launched the *CeeTee*, named for Claudia Tinsley, my new bride, from this very popular spot. Above the bridge the water upriver became fresher, and the catch might change from trout and spot tail bass to largemouth bass and red breast at any point. Below the Highway 17 bridge was salt water all the way to the Atlantic.

Since Claudia and I were mainly interested in learning how to catch big silver kings, as tarpon are called, we stayed below the bridge and followed the schooling tarpon all the way to the ocean and back.

For several weeks we caught very few fish, but our luck changed when we met Jim McVeigh, who lived in the fishing and shrimping community of Darien. From time to time he was a shrimper, commercial fisherman, crabber, and all-around Low Country waterman.

One afternoon in July, Claudia and I were bringing the *Cee-Tee* back in from an unproductive day of soaking fresh mullet for tarpon when we came upon Jim. His motor had died and he was drifting out the river on a rapidly falling tide. We asked if he needed help, which he did, and after introductions and then passing over of a stout rope, we towed Jim's boat back to Two-Way. During the tow in, we chatted about a lot of things including our hope to learn more about the fishing in the area and particularly how to catch the big silver kings.

After that initial meeting we did not see Jim again until a week later. Claudia and I had launched the *CeeTee* that morning at 8:00 A.M. and by 8:30 we were following a school of medium-size tarpon down the Altamaha. Jim pulled up alongside. Learning that we were seeing large schools of tarpon on almost every trip out but were not getting a strike, Jim asked how and where we had been fishing. As we floated along with the tide, gunwale to gunwale, we explained all we knew to do was find the deep holes in the river and bottom-fish with freshly cut mullet fillets. I told Jim we were so determined to learn about this type fishing that we had even entered the Big Tarpon Derby.

Jim advised, "It's time to try something a little different. Run out pretty close to the inlet, and when the tide turns, you'll notice that one big school of pogies after another will head upriver. Get the boat about forty to fifty feet ahead of one of those schools and troll, right in the school, with something that's bright, noisy, and creates a lot of motion. Troll at the same speed as the school, and try to keep the plug in the middle of it. Be patient and stay with the school. The water can be muddy so the tarpon have a hard time seeing individual baitfish."

"Jim," I asked, "what do you think would be a good plug?"

"Do you have some type of broken back medium running plug? You need something big, something with a lot of white on it."

Handing Claudia the controls, I began scrambling around in the two-tier wooden tackle box I had made. I pulled out a nine-inch-long red-and-white Creek Chub Pikie, a broken back plug with three sets of razor-sharp treble hooks.

"That'll work," Jim said. "Put it on with twelve inches of wire and an eight-foot double leader with a bimini twist. Troll slowly and stick with it. Those big fish feel more comfortable with a little more water under them. Toward the high tide the fishing will usually be best. Good luck and thanks for the tow last week."

Claudia stayed on the controls and kept a slow, steady course out the Altamaha River toward the ocean. The tide would turn about nine o'clock. We planned to follow Jim's instructions on the incoming water when the tide turned.

About the time I rigged up our two Fenwick rods, our friend Jack caught up with us in his boat. Jack and I were working at the Navy base together, running the testing office for the Federal Aviation Administration in the Air Traffic Control School at Glynco. The office was only open 8:00 to 5:00 o'clock five days a week, so Jack and I had gone fishing a lot together before I had married.

Jack put his engine in neutral and threw me a line. Drifting the outgoing tide, I filled him in on Jim's advice. He hunted for a blue-and-white Creek Chub in his collection. Once rigged up, we decided on the incoming water that Jack would troll to the left side of the river and that Claudia and I would take a school of pogies on the right. Making the turn at the ocean, I took the controls and put Claudia in the fighting chair. I waited for a big pod of pogie to leave for upriver, pulled ahead, matched their speed, and dropped in ahead of them.

The water was much clearer near the mouth of the river. The full moon made the tide higher than normal, which was pushing water upriver at a good clip. I took the rod from Claudia, checked the drag on the Penn reel, and felt good vibrations out of the plug at this speed. As I returned the rod, I cautioned Claudia to let me know if she felt the vibration change. The plug might have picked up trash. I also told her when she got a strike to put some muscle into the set.

A quarter ways upriver, Claudia got a good strike. This first ever tarpon strike really got us going. Jack, just off our port side and slightly ahead, saw the strike and gave us a thumbs-up.

Twenty minutes later Jack had a hook up with a six-foot tarpon clearing the water by at least three feet. It was so close to our boat when it jumped that I thought it might hit us as it splashed back into the water. Jack's fish threw his plug on the first jump. Disappointed and more than a little shaken at the size of the fish, Jack reeled in to check and reset his rig.

We later learned that we had been trolling through what the locals called Tarpon Alley.

Even though the strikes did not come quickly, the size of these fish made for very exciting fishing!

As soon as the menhaden – pogies they are called by most fishermen – left the ocean, the tarpon started following the school and gorging themselves on this plentiful hand-size bait in a feeding frenzy. Close to the back of the boat and all the way to the back of the school, huge tarpons rolled up out of the water. Then one of the silver kings crashed through the school and dozens of pogies on a life-or-death mission would shower into the air like so many missiles of mercury.

The excitement and adrenaline were intoxicating.

Twenty minutes further upriver Claudia suggested, "Let me drive. You take the rod awhile." We swapped places.

At 11:15 A.M. I hooked a smaller tarpon that turned out to be a real acrobat. I loosened the drag some and he jumped countless times. I played him very carefully, all the time coaching Claudia on how to handle the boat in the swift tide so that I could land this frisky fish.

About a half hour later I brought the tired fish along the starboard side and held it in the current. Pulling the gaff out of its holder on the transom and giving it to Claudia, I told her to put the boat in neutral. She slid the gaff under the tarpon's gill plate, and swung the fish aboard. Once we returned to the

Two-Way dock, we registered our first tarpon of the season. It was the first tarpon weighed for the Coastal Area Sport Fishing Tarpon Derby.

It was a red-letter day!

With the weather and tides again lining up in early August, we began seeing more and bigger tarpon in the pogie schools each day. I called Esther. With college graduation, my job with the navy, and a new wife in my life, I had not seen Esther for almost two years. When she arrived at our small apartment late on that August afternoon, she hadn't changed a bit. She was barefooted and tan as a chinaberry. She wore polarized black-rimmed glasses pushed back in her short curly hair, faded light-blue shorts, and an open collar cotton shirt. She and my new bride instantly became best friends.

As soon as we put Esther's canvas duffle in our second bedroom we grabbed the cooler and summer supper Claudia had put up and immediately headed to the marina. Claudia and I couldn't wait to show Esther the new boat we had spent fifteen months building. We were so proud of her.

At the marina, where the *CeeTee* sat on her trailer, I pulled off the cover, borrowed a tall ladder, and we all climbed aboard. Sitting in the boat we could see for miles across the green and gold saw grass marsh. Meandering cobalt creeks divided the marsh into many pieces, like a giant jigsaw puzzle. The western sun was low, and the late afternoon sea breeze kept the no-see-ums and mosquitoes far and away. Lounging in the new white captain chairs, bare feet on the gunwales, we ate fresh shrimp salad sandwiches and sipped on the champagne of the South – ice-cold sweet tea. Esther was impressed with every detail we had designed into the boat, and we swapped fishing stories until the rising full moon slipped above the horizon. Orange as a pumpkin, it overran the deep-purple dusk. In a contradiction of Mother Nature, as its size grew ever smaller, its brightness increased so that a tide chart could be read by its glow. We talked too late into the night, but the excitement and anticipation of the morrow had us at the Atlantic by 6:00 A.M.

At daybreak we picked up the first school and started upriver. The school of menhaden was enormous. In no time we were engulfed in ten times ten thousand. The tarpon, thick in the school, escorted our boat on every side. The fish were big and plentiful, but Esther got only one strike on both tides that first day.

Sunday the weather still held, but the water had turned muddy. I did not take this as a good omen, but we determined to be patient and stick with it.

The pogie schools were huge, it was hard to believe that so many fish could gather in one place. They covered what seemed to be acres. As the sun bolted out of the Atlantic to the east, the view over our transom toward the blazing horizon was a sea of chrome butterflies. The five-inch long menhaden, covered in polished platinum scales, rose at random out of the sea and danced on the surface for a second, only to be replaced with another, then another, and another. The scene was of metallic butterflies skittering on the water's surface with the piercing rays of the sun turning their fins and shimmering scales into fluttering silver wings. It was visual overload. We stared, mesmerized.

The spell was broken at 10:15 A.M. The hit came like a lightning bolt.

The six-foot tarpon was three feet above the water while Esther was still trying to react to his bone-jarring strike. Well over forty feet behind the boat, he looked hugenoxious on his second jump. In less than ten seconds he cut another full somersault. I caught a glimpse of the red-and-white plug planted firmly in the corner of his jaw as he pancaked back into the Altamaha.

Esther had caught up with him now. She had the slack out of the line and an arc in the heavy rod. She was a very experienced fisherman and unless something unusual happened, this trophy was hers. But that's why it's called fishing and not catching. Anything can happen with a heavy fish, and this one was a flyer. I kept the boat in the deepest part of the river, staying away from sandbars and snags. The rascal jumped six more times and kept us busy, but forty-five minutes later I turned the controls over to Claudia and slid the gaff gently through its gills. While I held his head slightly out of the water, Esther tied a line around his tail. The two of us muscled him over the gunwale.

We were only a mile at this point from the landing, so we wasted no time getting the old boy on a set of official scales. At Two-Way he weighed 88 pounds 8 ounces and was 69 inches long with a 32-inch girth. It was a beautiful fish. A real trophy. Esther quickly decided she wanted to have him mounted. A friend back at Georgetown was a good taxidermist and so after the weigh-in, picture taking, and many retellings of the story, Esther was on the pay phone to Georgetown getting instructions on where to ship the fish.

That's right. You heard me, ship the fish! In the early 1970s trophy fish were skin mounts, not made out of plastic like today; so the taxidermist needed the fish, the real fish, not just pictures and measurements.

Esther returned to the dock where we were all still showing off the trophy. When she announced she needed to get her fish shipped to Georgetown, the list of potential problems with this plan began to form in my mind and grew rapidly.

- Fish hanging on the scales in the August sun
- Temperature pushing 90° and it wasn't even lunchtime
- Scale reading 88 and a half pounds, tape measuring 68 inches long
- Fish not fitting in a car or our refrigerator
- Esther staying several more days

How were we going to get the fish to Georgetown? In a flash of genius the answer to all my questions came to me. We would mail it! Wasn't the United States Postal Service's motto "Neither snow nor rain nor heat nor gloom of night ..." No doubt they could handle a trophy tarpon.

But we had to get this fish out of the sun and quickly. I backed the boat under the scales and lowered Esther's prize onto the floorboards. We three jumped into my gray 1968 Chevrolet and towed the *CeeTee* down Highway 17 toward Glynco Naval Air Station as fast as the heavy Sunday traffic would allow.

An hour later I pulled up to the backdoor of the mess hall and luckily caught Don Wyland just as lunch for 500 or so black shoes was coming to a close. Don was Chief Petty Officer over the galley and I had taken him fishing several times. Don owed me one.

Now it was my time to do a little fishing.

I called out, "Don, come outside quick. I have to show you something you aren't going to believe!" I was baiting the hook.

Don followed me out to the trailered boat. "Jump up on the trailer fender and look at what we caught this morning," I prompted.

Don, with great anticipation, hopped up and holding onto the gunwale, peered over at the biggest fish he had ever seen. Don was from Iowa.

"Good gosh a'mighty! Where'd you catch that thing?" Don said with a mixture of reverence and longing in his voice.

"We caught it in Tarpon Alley, halfway from the ocean back toward Two-Way. Want to go up next week and try 'em?" I offered.

I was slowly trolling my bait through the water now.

"Man, you know it! I'd give anything to catch a fish like that."

I was about to catch the second biggest fish of the day.

"Don, we'll go next Saturday morning high tide," I promised. "But I need a little favor."

"You name it, buddy," Don said. "Anything!"

Strike!

"Well, my good friend Esther here caught this beautiful trophy. Most likely will win first place in the tarpon derby. Esther wants to have it mounted, but we must get it cold quickly so it won't spoil." I paused to let this detail sink in. Don, being a little slow on the uptake, scrunched up his eyes and furrowed his brow like he was trying to see something way off in the future. "Don," I added very slowly, "we need you to freeze the fish, hide it in your freezer for a few days 'til we get everything ready to mail it."

Very slow in his response, Don asked, "You want me to put that monster of a fish in the galley freezer until you mail it?"

"That's right, Don. I need a couple days to get everything ready. It would be a shame not to preserve such a beautiful trophy, don't you think? And Don, you're the only one who can help us."

Don slowly climbed back up on the trailer fender. He evaluated the fish now with a somewhat different eye. He inquired, "That is one heck of a fish! What does it weigh?"

"Just a little over eighty pounds. You and I can manage it, no trouble," I assured him.

"I'm trying to think how we can get it through the kitchen and into the freezer without anyone noticing," Don said.

Set the hook, fish on!

"Don, you're a real friend. Thanks so much. I've been thinking about that. Why don't we roll the fish up in one of those white cloths that make table covers, and you and I carry it straight through the kitchen. Anybody asks, you can tell 'em it's a side of prime beef for the next officers' club party. No one'll mess with it if you tell 'em that," I assured him.

Don went in, got the starched white tablecloth, and we spread it out in the bottom of the *CeeTee*. Esther and Claudia, standing on the fenders, alternated keeping lookout and monitoring our progress. Once the fabric was stretched out nice and straight, Don and I moved the fish to the edge and proceeded to roll it over and over toward the opposite side. Then we tucked the excess bottom material in just like the clerk does the butcher paper at the meat counter.

We left the top open so as to have a place to slip the meat hook under the fish's gill. The wet fish stuck skintight to the tablecloth. When we manhandled it over the gunwale and through the rear screen door, it looked, and, more importantly, smelled, just like a dead fish - which, of course, was not a real surprise.

No one in the kitchen seemed to pay much attention. The opened freezer door belched an icy fog as we slipped in. Once the fish was on the hook, Don draped the whole affair in a second tablecloth which disguised its shape magnificently.

Gaffed and landed, home free.

As Don closed the freezer door and glanced around the busy kitchen, he gave a sigh of relief and whispered, "If I ain't busted back to an E1 seaman this time, next week you and I are going fishing!"

"You're a buddy. Thanks. I'll call before we come back, maybe before you open for breakfast one morning."

"That would be best," agreed Don.

The next day I had to work. At lunchtime I went to the main post office on Glouster Street in Brunswick to see about size and weight limits and charges on shipping a crate. The man behind the worn Formica counter asked what I wanted to ship.

I nonchalantly answered, "A wooden crate."

"I mean," he said a little impatiently, "What's in the crate you're shipping?"

"Well, uh, uh, it's fish. A trophy – you know, a trophy fish," I hurried on. He wrote that down.

"How big is the crate?" he asked.

"Well, let's see. About 100 inches long, 16 inches wide, and, I would guess, 10 inches deep." He continued writing the details down on the same form, pushed the keys on his calculator, and pulled the handle to get the result. He mumbled, "8.6 cubic feet."

"What's the weight? Do you know?" he asked.

"I'd estimate one hundred pounds – crate and all."

He looked up, raised an eyebrow, and said, "That's a lot of fish."

"Yes sir, it is," I agreed.

I thought, *You have no idea!*

I then asked the key question, "Sir, (when you are but an E5 in the Navy you call everybody sir), could you tell me how long it would take to ship my crate to Georgetown, South Carolina?"

He looked briefly at some chart taped to the fading green countertop, then looked up and said, "Two to five days. Depends on the amount of freight we have going out."

I thought, *Two's okay; five is going to be a push.*

"What are the best days to ship to get it there quickly," I asked.

Without hesitation he answered, "Wednesday."

This was encouraging news. Today was Monday.

"Where do I bring the crate to unload it?" was my next question.

"Just drive around back. It loops all the way around to the next street so it's no problem getting in or out," he explained.

"Thank you, sir." I hurried back to work and asked my immediate supervisor, a marine master sergeant, if I could get off a half-hour early so I could go by the lumberyard. With permission granted, I picked up two sheets of half-inch plywood, wood glue, and nails. That evening while Claudia cooked up a pot of shrimp mull, Esther and I built a crate for the fish out on our ground floor apartment's patio. After supper, while it was still good light, we headed for the island market and bought all the leftover newspapers from that morning.

Tuesday morning before breakfast I stopped by the galley, went in the back door, and asked Don if I could take a peek in the freezer. We both slipped in and I pushed on the tablecloth-draped tarpon. It was almost frozen. By next morning it would be solid as a rock.

As I departed I assured Don I would be at the backdoor by 5:30 A.M. so we could load the fish. He seemed very relieved.

That night I checked the crate. The glue was dry, the top fit just perfectly, the address in Georgetown was printed clearly on the lid. The newspapers had been separated into single sheets ready to wrap up the frozen fish for preservation.

Next morning Claudia, Esther, and I got up before light and drove across the Saint Simons causeway to Glynco. We pulled up to the backdoor of the galley at 5:30 A.M. sharp. I opened the trunk of the Impala and spread out the canvas cover I had borrowed off the boat. Don and I quickly hoisted the tarpon off its hook and, as quickly as possible, eased through the kitchen's stainless steel mixers and ovens, right out the screen door. We gently loaded our prize onto the tarp in the trunk of my car. The tail was sticking out some.

After Don removed his two tablecloths, the four of us stood there a minute looking at the great fish. Once again Don admired its size and in a hushed voice captured our thoughts, "That's a heck of a trophy."

I thanked him and the three of us rushed back across the causeway. I backed the Impala into the parking space closest to our apartment. Claudia went in the front door to open the sliding glass doors out to the backyard while Esther and I hoisted the fish out of the trunk, through the kitchen and living room, and onto the patio. We had already put four or five layers of newspaper on the bottom and sides to line the crate.

In went the fish. The remaining newspaper was spread out over the top of the fish and crumpled up and stuffed between the fish and the sides. I nailed the top of the crate on, and we carried the now-loaded crate out to the car, stuck it in as far as it would go, and tied the lid of the trunk down.

A quarter to eight. I kissed Claudia goodbye and shook hands with Esther, telling her I would call her at Pawleys in a few days to be sure her trophy arrived.

I arrived at the backdoor to the post office on Glouster Street right at their opening time of 8:30 A.M. I went up the backsteps and was first in line at the counter. The same gentleman that had helped me was there and I told him if he had someone to help me we could get the crate that we had discussed a few days before, out of my car. It wasn't but a minute and a young man met me at the car to help me set the crate on the scales. The slender black pointer settled at 105 pounds. The young man hollered out, "105, Jake," as I returned to the counter.

Jake figured up the freight. It came to $19.28. As I was getting a twenty out of my starched, white thirteen-button pants, I asked Jake if he thought the crate would go out today. He looked over at the stack of boxes ready to be loaded on the freight truck that morning and offered, "I'm afraid not. We have a heavy load today which is unusual, so it probably won't go until tomorrow or even Friday."

Thursday might mean a Saturday delivery, four days. Friday would mean all the way to Monday morning, a sixth day. Nothing about our packing was going to hold a fish six days in August heat. Panic set in.

I put on my best manners. "Sir," I said, "that shipment is for a very special lady friend of mine in Georgetown. Is there anything at all you could do to get that crate on the truck today?"

Jake looked up from his paperwork, sized me up and down, and finally smiled. Looking over his shoulder out back, he promised, "As soon as I complete your shipping papers and before I go on my coffee break, I'll personally mark your crate PERISHABLE.

"Perishable?" I asked. I had the horrible thought, *This man can read my mind.*

"Yes, perishable," Jake explained. "That will mean they will load it out first this morning."

With that calming bit of assurance, I drove on to work.

On Friday afternoon I dialed Esther's number on the fishing pier at Pawleys Island. Someone answered it on the third ring and I heard the voice completing a transaction, "That'll be $2.50 for the bait and sinkers." Then the voice hollered, "Hey, Esther, it's for you." Back to the customer again, the voice directed, "Try over on the left side about the second wave out. Seem to be biting best there right now." Again the voice shouted, "Esther, the phone's for you!"

When Esther got to the phone I asked how her trip going back home was. What were the fish doing off the pier? Finally, did her tarpon arrive in good shape?

Esther replied, "Johnny, the fish isn't here. What day did you ship it?" I told her I shipped it Wednesday morning, and it was almost guaranteed to be there by Friday afternoon.

She said, "I'll call the post office right now and see if they have the crate."

I did not hear back from Esther until Sunday morning. Claudia and I fished a late tide Friday night and all day Saturday. Late Sunday Esther called. With a little panic in her voice she said the post office had not received anything for her on Friday or Saturday.

"Esther, that can't be good. I'll check with the post office here first thing in the morning."

Knowing that 90 pounds of frozen fish had gone missing for six days made me calculate my telephone inquiry with an abundance of caution. I waited until first break Monday morning, went to the pay phone out in the breakroom, dropped my dime in, and called the main downtown post office in Brunswick. A lady answered. I was very relieved it was not Jake, as I was afraid he might recognize my voice.

I, as casually as possible, said, "I was just checking on a shipment that I was expecting at my house on Pawleys Island. I believe it was shipped on Wednesday of last week. Would you be so kind as to check on it for me?"

"Hold a minute," the voice said. Long two minutes later. "Your name Esther Johnson?"

"No ma'am, but I am a friend of hers and she asked me to call," I offered.

"Please write this phone number down. Have Miss Johnson call me. There's a problem with her shipment," the post mistress said.

I dutifully wrote the phone number down and hesitantly asked, "So can I tell her something? Could you tell me the nature of the problem?" I asked.

With a little chuckle, she said, "Well, I guess it can't hurt. The manager here when the crate came in got a call from his wife that she was fixing to have their baby. He dashed out before he completed the shipping papers. Without any paperwork, the temporary guy stacked the crate on the mezzanine above the office. Whatever was in the crate spoiled over the weekend, and all that mess oozed through the mezzanine floor, then through the ceiling tiles, and onto the service desk and front counter. No one can work in the office for the smell. I am talking to you from the phone on the loading dock. The smell is so bad we had to send everyone else home. We're borrowing a truck from the fish market to haul that crate off so we don't ruin one of our trucks, too. The cleanup crew says it might be the end of the week before we can come back to work, and that depends on if we haul off the desks and buy new ones. Looks like this could run $10,000. Please tell Miss Johnson to call me at that number so we can tell her we're sorry about her shipment. Say, while I got you on the phone, how about giving me your name and phone number?"

Click. I eased the receiver back on the hook. I was taking no chances.

Later that day I called Esther to give her the bad news. She took it well. By the time the euphoria of catching the fish had worn off, she had checked on the cost of the mounting and also figured out she did not have anywhere big enough in her trailer to hang the trophy.

She was not too upset. We had taken some great pictures.

A small article in *The Brunswick News* next morning stated the main post office would be closed for at least a week. Further down in the article the damage was estimated at around $10,000.

For the rest of my three-year tour in Brunswick, I never showed my face near that post office again.

In October the newspaper announced that Miss Esther Johnson of Pawleys Island, South Carolina, had won first place in the Coastal Area Sport Fishing Tarpon Derby. They ran a nice picture of Esther and her fish along with the article. Esther did receive in the mail a beautiful trophy.

After that, every time Claudia and I visited Esther we smiled as we looked at that impressive trophy sitting on top of her television set. All of us laughed about what we called from that day on, the $10,000 tarpon.

FOR PAY FISHING

As I eased the 1987 pale blue Oldsmobile station wagon up the steep, narrow winding dirt road, mountain laurel and the tips of soft hemlock branches brushed the sides of the car. This was no main thoroughfare. As the little road penetrated the green tunnel and we drew further from the tar-and-gravel state-maintained highway, scenes from the movie *Deliverance* flashed through my subconscious.

The small hand-lettered sign at the entrance touted FOR PAY FISHING. The FISHING was followed by the familiar dollar sign, but the S in the abbreviation for United States was backwards. Fishing sounded like an idea that had some possibilities for entertaining the two energetic nine-year-olds in the backseat.

My son, John, and his best friend, Scott Neely, were sky-high on adrenaline, having just won their 9 A.M. soccer match in the first game of their regional tournament held in Waynesville, North Carolina. The winners of that morning's first game were not scheduled to play again until 4 o'clock that afternoon. So I had the task of keeping two young boys, still in their soccer uniforms, busy and out of trouble for more than four hours.

In Spartanburg County where we lived, I had seen pay fishing ponds, but had never visited one. Even so, I had a decidedly

185

negative impression of them. Undistinguished species like cat-fish, carp, and the occasional gar were heavily advertised as "stocked regularly." The pay ponds I had observed were little more than scooped out, man-made holes in the ground filled with muddy water. In general they were a poor excuse as a place for fish to live.

This second Saturday of the Thanksgiving month we were a hundred miles from home in unfamiliar territory, and the fishing sign was the best offer we had come across. So fishing for pay it was to be.

The last sharp bend in the road brought us out into what local folks in the Blue Ridge Mountains of North Carolina call a cove – any reasonably flat piece of land lying between two moun-tains. Unlike a valley, a cove is usually open only on one end. This one fit the description.

As we exited the wood line, in front of us was an unpreten-tious clapboard cabin nestled between the mountains toenailed to the last piece of buildable land. At one time the cabin may have been painted white. A tiny bold stream tumbled into the upper end of a beautiful, natural half-acre pond that substituted for what passed for the cabin's front yard. I would have bet that the water temperature, clear as air, would have been south of sixty-five degrees.

My hopes rose several notches.

I noticed at the right side of the pond a lean-to with a rusty corrugated tin roof. It apparently served as the office of the fish-ing enterprise.

After I parked near the lean-to, the boys scrambled out. I slammed my door extra hard in hopes of notifying someone of our arrival. Standing in the stillness of the mountain morning, I could hear the unmistakable sound of someone splitting firewood. From the steady rhythm of the axe hitting wood and the sound of twin blocks falling to either side of the chopping block, I didn't think this a novice effort. We did not have to wait long for the one-gallused woodcutter to appear from behind the most distant of the scattered outbuildings. Our host greeted us. He was a two hundred-fifty pounder with the fitness and tanned weathered skin of a person who makes his living outdoors. A broad smile accentuated his full salt-and-pepper beard. An involuntary sigh of relief escaped my lips as I relaxed a little.

This man, apparently very glad to see us, wore faded denim coveralls and a blue and white checkered flannel shirt. The tag right above the narrow pencil pocket on the front of the coverall read Oshkosh. As his ham-sized calloused right hand swallowed mine, he said, "Name's Tucker, Tucker Blackwood." He glanced over at the two boys and inquired, "Come to try your luck?"

As I followed his glance toward the boys, I saw them already scampering up and down the lush green grassy banks of the pond like two wild, frisky colts.

I explained, "Yes, we have. We've some time between soccer games over in Waynesville, and the boys would like to try their hand with the fish."

"Well, that's fine, just fine. We only raise brown trout. If that's okay, bring your rods on over to the shed, and we'll get you started."

The "only raise brown trout" lifted my hopes to the heights of a school-age boy initiating a substitute teacher, but the "bring your rods over" caught me a little off guard.

"Well, uh, Tucker, we didn't bring any fishing gear, I'm afraid. Didn't know we would be going fishing," I offered. Just when I was beginning to hope the boys might actually catch a fish or two, I realized all of a sudden that the lack of fishing gear seemed a potential stumbling block.

Tucker's smile broadened a little more. He said, "You're in luck! I have a couple of rods and reels for rent."

With another wave of relief, I followed Tucker over to the lean-to, which sheltered a counter made from a weathered twelve-inch board nailed across the front between two 4x4s. I stopped at the front of the counter as Tucker disappeared into the gloom of the lean-to. As he rummaged around, I could hear the hum of an ice maker with a bad bearing. On a shelf behind the counter was a line of new, unopened, shiny tin cans containing whole yellow corn.

Briefly, Tucker reappeared proudly holding two well-used Sears & Roebuck mail order fiberglass rods with closed-face Zebco reels. The rods were loaded with 20-pound monofilament line, a small split-shot sinker, and a long shank gold-plated hook.

"These two should work fine for the boys. Did you want one also?" Tucker asked.

"No, no, just the ones for the two boys will be fine," I replied.

"How much are the rods?" I asked.

"Well, the rods are $2.50 per hour. The fee for fishing is $2.50 per hour, plus $2.50 per fish," Tucker explained. With a smile best described as beaming, he added, "Oh, and a can of corn for each boy is free!"

All in all a very fair deal, I thought.

I had taken the boys pond fishing for bass and bream enough times to know they liked fishing, and if they caught a trout or two that would be icing on the cake. Tucker expertly whipped the top off two cans of corn using a rusty can opener screwed to one of the 4x4 supports. Once I had reviewed with the boys briefly how the Zebco reels worked, Tucker demonstrated how to put at least two kernels of corn on the gold hooks. This part was new. Neither of the boys had fished for trout before, and I had never fished for trout with anything but a fly rod. I did not know trout have a deep affection for whole yellow corn. I determined this bit of information might come in handy in future situations.

The boys each grabbed a can and rod and headed to the far end of the pond. At this point I fully expected Tucker to return to his chores. As I said, "Thanks, I think we got it," Tucker smiled, "I'll be glad to stay and help the boys."

I wondered how much help I needed with just two boys who knew enough to bait their own hooks. I could certainly lend them a hand if they happened to catch a fish. Before this thought was dry on the paper, Scott yelled, "I got one!" We all looked as one in Scott's direction to see him holding on with both hands to his rod, sharply bent, the line melting off the reel which seemed to have a surprisingly smooth drag. About the middle of the pond the trout, a beautiful healthy brown, cleared the surface by a foot and splashed down as only a chunky two-pounder can.

"Bring a net!" Scott hollered.

A net? "You got a net?" I asked Tucker, never taking my eyes off Scott and his fish.

"Yep," Tucker beamed, "I happen to also rent nets. $2.50 an hour."

"Just add one to my bill," I said. Before I could get the words out of my mouth, I felt Tucker place the wooden handle in my hand as I ran down the bank to help Scott. Since Scott was my guest, I did not want him to lose this first fish. I raced toward Scott – who was beginning to win the battle – thinking, *This is great! A very respectable fish early in the day will keep both boys' interest up for the rest of the afternoon.*

About the time I reached Scott, John hollered out, "Dad, I've got one, too! Hurry! Bring the net!"

Tucker, I realized, was paying close attention and appeared quickly at John's side with a second net. John's fish did a complete somersault about twenty yards from the bank, suggesting that, if anything, it was even bigger than Scott's.

Boy, I thought, *this is too wonderful! Two nice fish in five minutes. What a great idea this was!*

Scott's fish glided toward the bank on its side. I slid the net under it and laid it out on the emerald grass to remove the hook. He had caught a real beauty.

"Scott, just wait here. My camera is in the car. Let's take a picture of your first fish," I said.

Passing John as I ran to the car, I could see he was having a good fight out of his fish. I shouted over my shoulder as I went by, "Don't horse him. Keep your rod tip up. Let him run if he wants to."

I grabbed my camera off the dashboard and headed back toward Scott. On the run, I ripped open the box, tore off the aluminum foil wrapper, and wound the thumbscrew to advance the film. Kodak had just come out with these new disposable cameras and I had purchased several at the drugstore in hopes of getting some good pictures of the soccer team.

After reaching Scott, we removed his fish from the net, making sure he held the fish broadside and out in front as far as possible. I learned this old fisherman's trick to taking flattering photos of bragging-size fish long ago. "Hold still Scott, let me get one more shot," I said.

"Mr. Faris, can I keep him?" Scott asked.

"Sure, bring him on down, and we'll help John get his fish in too."

By the time we reached John's side of the pond, Tucker was happily sliding his net under John's brownie. I took a couple pictures of John's fish and then a snapshot of both boys holding their two nice-sized trout.

"Dad, what do you think they weigh?" John asked.

"I don't know, but they are both really nice trout. Tucker, you got some scales we could weigh the fish on?" I asked.

"Sure thing. We'll weigh 'em and put 'em in a wire box in the creek to keep them cool."

Tucker laid the fish one at a time on waxed butcher's paper and weighed them on a set of old meat market scales.

The dial settled on two-and-a quarter for Scott's fish, and two-and-three-quarter pounds on John's. Both fish – beautifully colored, fat, and healthy – would be delicious cooked on the grill. In less than thirty minutes, the boys had caught two trout. They were very excited and having a good time. Quickly I mentally added up $2.50 each for the rods, $2.50 each for the hour of fishing, $2.50 times two for the fish, and $2.50 for the net. With the two cans of corn at no charge, that came to $17.50.

1 Hour Fishing x 2 Fishermen at $2.50/Hour	$ 5.00
Rod Rental for 1 Hour x 2 Rods at $2.50/Hour	$ 5.00
Net Rental Fee for 1 Hour at $2.50/Hour	$ 2.50
2 Trout at $2.50/Each	$ 5.00
	$17.50

Best money I ever spent, I thought.

"Okay, let's see if you can catch some more," Tucker smiled as he dropped both fish into the live well which he had fashioned to just fit into the cold water of the feeder creek.

Scott and John both baited up and cast out about a third of the way into the pond. Before their sinkers even carried their hooks to the bottom - bam! - they had a doubleheader. The boys, now displaying more confidence, brought both fish to net in half the time.

It was obvious the line test on their two reels was sized to catch fish. Worrying about breaking off a fat, frisky fish was not even a thought. Same drill – net the fish, pose for picture, weigh the fish (this time John's two-and-one-half and Scott's almost three), and add them to the live well.

Big smiles covered everyone's faces. Tucker seemed to really enjoy the action, too. Before the first hour was spent, the boys had caught and weighed in eight fish. Scott had five and John three to his credit.

I had been fishing a lot of years, but this trip was rivaling some of the fastest fishing I had ever experienced.

As Scott and John baited up, Tucker eased up to me and quietly asked, "Want to fish another hour?"

"Sure thing, the boys are having a ball and their game's not until four. It'll only take us an hour to get back, so we have until three o'clock. We'll fish as long as they want," I said. Tucker's grin was so hard I'm sure it hurt his face.

As I watched the boys, John missed a strike and reeled his line in to check if his corn was gone. When his hook was still two feet down, I could see in the crystal clear water that the bright hook was empty. With one more turn of the reel, a three-pounder smacked the flashing empty gold hook.

As John set the hook, he exclaimed, "Wow! Dad, did you see that? There wasn't even any bait on the hook and that big trout whacked it!"

Scott was fast into another rod bender.

For the first time a little bell went off in the back of my head, and I subconsciously began figuring up the potential tab. Two hours fishing times two, $10.00. Rent on two rods, $10.00. Net rental for two hours, $5.00. Fish caught, eight times $2.50 each.

2 Hours Fishing x 2 Fishermen at $2.50/Hour	$10.00
Rod Rental for 2 Hours x 2 Rods at $2.50/Hour	$10.00
Net Rental Fee for 2 Hours at $2.50/Hour	$ 5.00
8 Trout at $2.50/Each	<u>$20.00</u>
	$45.00

Total $45.00, and the boys were both struggling with the next two fish.

As I grabbed the net to help land numbers nine and ten, a little voice in the back of my mind was saying, "*Do you have enough cash? They don't take checks up in these mountains!*" This thought was interrupted as Tucker eased up to me again and inquired, "Are you going to want me to clean the fish for you?"

As I bent down and slid the net under Scott's sixth two-plus pounder, I called over my shoulder, "Sure, Tucker, that would be great! Thanks very much."

Tucker figured, "I think I'll get started and fix them as we go 'stead of waiting 'til the end." He quickly added, "Runs $2.50 per fish filleted and wrapped. How many fillets you want in a package?"

Laying Scott's fish in the grass, I directed, "Let's do two per pack."

Tucker hurried off. From my location around the pond I could soon hear him humming as he worked away cleaning fish. He was struggling to keep up.

Two o'clock came and went. The boys continued to hook a fish just about every throw now. I kept busy netting them and taking pictures until we ran out of film at 2:45 P.M. A few minutes before three I figured my bill was somewhere close to $185.00! Holy cow!

Between netting fish numbers twenty-nine and thirty, I slipped my wallet out to see how much cash I had left. I had brought extra in case the team won and we had to stay over. A quick count came to $240.00. I figured we could get home on $8 worth of gas and $10 for burgers, but it would be close. If we won the next game at 4:00 and needed to spend the night, I had a problem. This was long before I owned a credit card.

I called a halt exactly at three. I hollered to the boys, "Let's go. Time to hit the road."

Both almost in unison said, "Just one more, please!"

"No, no, not another fish. Let's go." I insisted.

When we got to the lean-to I returned the well-used net. The boys put their hooks in the base of the first ferrule and wound their lines up tight so the rods would be ready for the next customers.

Tucker, just folding the butcher paper on the last package of fillets and fastening it with freezer tape, said, "Bring your cooler on over. We'll weigh the fillets and load them."

I thought a second and said, "Tucker, I didn't bring a cooler, do you have one?"

"No problem. Just happen to have some for sale. They're $5.00 each. Are you going to need ice? It's $2.50 for ten pounds."

"Yes," I said, "we'll need both." My mind was trying to calculate the added cost.

Tucker tore off the lid to a carton of Jolly Green Giant Niblets corn and pulled a pencil out of his bib overalls. "Now let me see," he said.

He began listing the gear we had rented.

"That's…"

3 hours fishing x 2 fishermen at $2.50/hour	$ 15.00
Rod rental for 3 hours x two rods at $2.50/hour	$ 15.00
Net rental for 3 hours at $2.50/hour	$ 7.50
32 Trout at $2.50/each	$ 80.00
Cleaning and wrapping at $2.50/fish	$ 80.00
(1) Cooler at $5.00	$ 5.00
(1) 10 pound bag ice at $2.50/bag	$ 2.50
	$205.00

Tucker straightened up, studied his box top full of cyphering carefully, and said, "That comes to $205.00. Hmmm, tell you what, let's just call it $200 even."

As I counted out the bills and rechecked to see how much I had left, the boys loaded the cooler in the back of the station wagon. All in all, I had $40 in my pocket, a cooler full of prime trout fillets, and two beaming young fishermen. However at $66.67 per hour, I doubted that we would return any time soon to For Pay Fishing.

FIRST DEER

The green sign with white letters read Durango, Colorado, Population 2165. I pulled our pale blue 1987 Oldsmobile station wagon with imitation wood grain siding into an open parking place outside a wood frame building – Mountain Outfitters.

We were done; all four of us were ready to take a break. We were averaging four hundred miles per day on this, our last of four family western trips. Another hundred miles still lay ahead of us this day, but we all needed to escape the car and each other for a while. My wife and Ashley, our fifteen-year-old daughter, headed to a western clothing store across the hot, dusty street while John, our twelve-year-old, and I entered the manufactured cool of a large hunting and fishing outfitter. The weathered wooden façade resembled a saloon in a black-and-white western movie.

Rows of domestic- and foreign-made rifles, racks of beautifully crafted fly rods, and aisles of tents and camping gear in all colors, shapes, and sizes spread before us. We both eyed, with more than a little envy, trophy mule deer, elk, bear, moose, salmon, rainbow trout, and antelope mounts that covered the upper portion of the walls. But it was the bow section that stopped my young son and held him captive.

Before the end of the half-hour rest stop, I had purchased for John a secondhand Browning junior compound bow. I believe it was the highlight of the entire two- week trip for John. After returning home the first week in August, not a Saturday went by without John begging to go to the Totem Pole in Union, South Carolina, a small rural town, ten miles from our farm in the Piedmont section of our state.

It might be good to explain here that deer hunting was just becoming popular in the Upstate. The region had not had a deer population very long, but thanks to the Fish and Game folk's stocking program twenty years earlier, Union County now had a respectable population. Within our group of hunting buddies, at least once a season, a nice buck would give someone bragging rights.

John and I had only recently caught the deer hunting fever. I had killed my very first buck only the year before, a respectable six-pointer. John had decided that instead of hunting deer with a rifle, he would take on the added challenge of bow hunting.

Being complete novices about this primitive hunting technique, John and I sought out the Totem Pole, a unique backyard establishment, which had the reputation of "fixing you up with all you need." The store's owner adjusted the bow to John's arm and draw length and custom-made him half-a-dozen arrows with camouflage shafts and yellow and green fletching. We acquired arrow points for practicing as well as razor-sharp broadheads of the same weight that you screwed into the shaft when practice was over and the real show began.

An hour on the store's in-house practice range gave us enough confidence to head home; John full of anticipation, me with a smile on my face at the fun my son was having.

John did not miss a day during the next six weeks without spending all his spare time with his bow. I had stacked and tied fifty new, flat corrugated boxes together to make an archery target in the basement for John's practice. With the target placed at the farthest corner of the unfinished room and John backed up to the opposite wall, he had enough room to get off a good fifteen-yard shot. This was enough distance to rehearse for the shot he was training for once deer season opened.

During this time John and I traveled to our small farm every Sunday after church and scouted a good place to hang a stand. Luck came about two weeks before the season opened on September 15, when the two of us were walking through a hardwood drainage that encompassed our small duck pond. John was seriously looking for fresh rubs and scrapes while I enjoyed my time with him and the shower of beautiful tobacco, red, and orange fall leaves.

John's search carried him up the steep right side of the drainage through a small group of mature white oaks and beech trees. Near the rim he hit the mother lode!

Beneath the low-hanging limbs of a spreading beech tree was the largest scrape either of us had ever seen on our land – a forty-inch irregular circle of perfectly cleared, black, loamy dirt. The mature buck that had recently passed this way had pawed the ground and swept it of all leaves. In this hardwood section of the woods with a layer of newly fallen leaves, the clear spot stood out like a neon light. Above the scrape the old buck had either chewed or torn off the tip of every branch within reach, leaving his scent to warn all lesser contenders that he intended to mate with every hot doe in these parts. Fifteen yards to the left of this spot we would hang John's climbing stand when the big day came.

Our unusual discovery and the accumulating anticipation of the season's opening was about to drive my son to distraction. Practice hours increased, study time took a backseat, and grades suffered. Opening weekend of bow season came and went, as did the following weekend. I could not get off work to take my young William Tell to the woods.

To his credit, John did not complain; but I knew how disappointed he was. Having to work on the first two weekends of the bow season was about to kill me. The third weekend I again had to work, this time traveling to a company trade show in Myrtle Beach, two hundred miles from our home. The show ran all day Thursday, Friday, and until lunch on Saturday. I wanted so badly to be off Saturday to take John hunting, but the likelihood of that working out looked slim.

Before leaving on Wednesday afternoon, however, I promised my twelve-year-old that I would get home as soon as I could. Maybe, just maybe, if at all possible, we could be at the farm for an hour or so before dark on Saturday.

At the end of the show Saturday morning, I took down and packed the display in the backseat of my car and hurried up I-26 at top speed. Close to home I found a phone booth and called John, telling him to get dressed and have all his gear ready when I pulled in the driveway. He could jump in, and we would head straight to the farm. The relief, gratitude, and excitement were evident in his words, "I'll be ready, Dad. Thanks."

Breaking most of South Carolina's speed limit laws landed me in the driveway a few minutes after four. John was standing in the yard just as he had promised. We drove as fast as the Crown Victoria would travel on the two-lane tar-and-gravel road the fifteen miles to the farm.

I was still wearing my business clothes – white dress shirt, striped tie, gray slacks, and shined penny loafers when we pulled up to the barn. No matter. I grabbed John's climbing stand out of the barn, threw it in the trunk of my Ford sedan, and drove, yes, drove, through the field of broom straw to within fifty yards of the woods' edge where we had seen the monster scrape.

John collected his bow and arrows, and I grabbed the stand. To our delight, the scrape was clean as a whistle and no doubt just recently freshened by Mr. Wall Hanger.

I slipped both sections of the climbing stand around a good straight hickory tree about eleven inches in diameter and helped John into the stand. I waited at the base of the tree until John had manipulated the stand up fifteen feet, turned around, secured the safety belt, and gotten settled. I passed his bow with four arrows in the quiver to him, all with new broadheads tightly screwed into the shafts. I whispered, "Good luck," and "Be careful," then eased the car back the quarter-mile to the barn.

By the time I parked the Crown Vic back at our rust-colored barn, the long shadows of late afternoon had almost reached John's side of the field. It had been a beautiful fall day with temperatures climbing to the low sixties. The rolling hills and woods of the farm were now accentuated by the fading western light. My location on the ridge in the middle of the old farm, and the land's rise from the edge of the hardwoods kept me from seeing John or anything that might cross the field in his direction.

Twelve years old, only twelve, and my son was fifteen feet off the ground, standing up in a climbing stand for the very first time, with four razor-sharp arrows, any one designed to cut the heart out of a two-hundred pound buck. I could not even see where he was from where I sat and in a handful of minutes it would be dark. What in the world was I thinking? My only consolation was, I knew there was no other place he would rather be. He loved it. John loved the outdoors. He loved it all and he got it honestly. He was growing up and I knew I had to let him go. Still I said a father's prayer.

As I sat on the loading ramp of the barn and fretted, I confess I did not really have much expectation that any deer would approach within shooting range of John's stand. We had been very late getting to the farm, had to drive across the fields to beat the clock, and had made a good bit of racket setting up the stand. No yearling, much less a wise mature buck, would be anywhere near that part of the farm after all that commotion. If John even got to spot a distant deer this evening, I would count it a huge blessing, but I still hoped. For John's sake, I still hoped.

The sun slipped behind the tall pines to the west. As a chill rose off Fairforest Creek, I tried to remember if anything in my suitcase would fit over my thin cotton shirt. The long-sleeved top to my pj's came to mind. I yanked my suitcase out from under the show displays piled in the backseat and slipped the pajama top over my shirt, necktie, and all. The thought briefly crossed my mind that my pale yellow top, tie, and dress slacks would look more than a little out of place in this setting, but who – except an old blue heron laboring overhead to roost – would ever be a witness?

Now it was every hunter's magic moments, the twenty minutes to dark. Purple dusk oozed in and melted into night.

Unlike a rifle, a bow told no story of the hunt. I waited until the thumbnail of a new moon tipped the treetops over my son's position before heading down in the car to pick him up. I only used the parking lights until I came close to his stand. Then I pulled the headlight knob on the dashboard, lighting up the woods with my low beams. To make John's descent safer, I flicked on the bright high beam lights.

In their glare was my twelve-year-old, bouncing up and down in his stand and pumping both arms, bow held over his head. John's grin seemed to cover his entire face. He was so excited, I felt sure he must have seen a deer, which would totally make his day, and mine, as well.

With the car running and lights burning, I hurried through the knee-high broom straw. He dropped me his bow and started shimmying down the tree. I noted, even before he hit the ground, only three arrows remained in the quiver – not four.

"Dad, I got him! I got him!" he whispered. "I got him! He stepped right in the scrape, and I shot him."

"Did you hit the deer, John?"

"Yes, sir! He was standing still. I shot him right where you told me to aim. Dad, he's big! He's really big!"

"Which way did he go?" I glanced over John's head, searching the area where the car lights fell.

"He went straight down the hill and out into the backwater, Dad. I could hear water splashing for a second or two. Then it all got quiet. He may have made it to the duck pond."

Much darker now, neither moonlight nor starlight would reach the floor of the swamp. We were totally unprepared for this scenario.

I thought for a second then said, "Let's ride back up to the barn and get the gas lantern."

We rode the short distance back up to the barn, then unlocked and rolled up the heavy door. I pulled the lantern from its hook on the wall, dusted it off, adjusted the gas, and lit the mantle with one of the big kitchen matches I kept in a glass jar. The lantern hissed to life. Assured the lantern had survived the hot summer months in good shape, I turned it off, grabbed a couple extra matches, and returned to the car.

An old logging road took us close to the deer's last position. When I reached where the little-used dirt road that crossed the head of the duck pond, I stopped, leaving the engine running and the lights on. After relighting the lantern and adjusting the flame to its brightest, John and I eased off the road into the head of the low, damp ground leading toward the headwaters of the pond.

Two thoughts crossed my mind: assuming he had made as good a shot as he had said, *I must find John's deer, after all it was his very first.*

And *My dress clothes were going to get really wet and really muddy.*

John moved out far to the right as the lantern beam spread, while I moved directly into the swamp. I held the Coleman lantern as high as I could so as to see past its bright beam. Wherever a small tuft of grass grew, I tried to step on that, knowing this would be higher ground than the wet, muddy spots. No matter. In minutes water had thoroughly soaked my shoes, socks, and britches legs. I could hear John splashing along ahead of me, oblivious to the fact that I was not protected by hand-me-down 18-inch L.L. Bean rubber boots, as he was.

When I reached the point where the light touched deeper backwater, I grew a little worried. Either John or I should have cut the deer's trail. Neither of us had seen blood or fresh tracks.

"John, you see anything?" I called out.

"No, Dad, nothing yet."

"Do you think he made it this far?"

"I don't know. I heard him splashing through water. But then all noise stopped, and I couldn't hear anything."

"Let's go back the way we came and move closer to the base of the hill. We'll make another pass."

"Okay, Dad," I heard from the fringe of light.

As I turned to head back myself, I stopped when a glint of reflected light caught my eye. What looked like just the base of a small sapling held my attention. I realized it was the curved antler of John's buck with its head lying on its side. John's prize was a buck, alright. A nice one from the look of it.

"John, I've got him spotted! He's between us. Start walking toward my voice."

The splashing of John's boots stopped suddenly. His excited voice called out, "I see him, Dad! I see him! He's lying in the muddy water."

The two of us reached the old rascal at the same time. We just stood there for a moment, looking at what was obviously a mature eight-pointer.

John eased to the ground and ran his hand all the way down the deer's side, patting him along the smooth mixture of brown and gray. The arrow, half broken, had sliced the deer's heart in two. The bruiser was dead on its feet but had powered through fifty yards before piling up.

"Great shot, son. Very clean. He's a very nice buck," I said.

We each grabbed one side of his antlers and started toward the car. Dragging the deer through the muck was tough going. The mud sucked a loafer right off my foot at one point, but after locating it, I slapped it back on and sloshed on toward the road.

Now what were we going to do?

"John, I don't think we have any choice but to put the deer into the trunk. That's the only place big enough to carry him to the processor. I don't know of another way to get him there. You stay here with the lantern and deer while I drive back up to the barn. I'll find something to lay him on. We'll ruin the car if we don't."

At the barn I found an old 10 foot x 10 foot tan canvas tarp, which I spread out, being sure to turn up all the edges to keep mud and blood off the carpet. I hurriedly drove back to my son and the deer.

Lifting the heavy deer up and over the edge of the bumper was like lifting jelly. As soon as we got one end in the trunk and then tried to push in the other end, the whole deer would flop out on the ground. After a few unsuccessful tries, I got in the trunk myself. I thought that if John could manage to lift one of the deer's front legs, maybe I could pull the rest of the deer up. After climbing in, I leaned out as far as possible while John struggled to hoist one of the deer's legs up to me. After several exhausting tries, I was able to snatch one foot as John lifted with all his might. I could do no more, though, than get the front half of the deer over the edge.

"John, you're going to have to climb in the trunk, too, so that we can both pull."

I held onto the front legs as John scrambled in with me. Once inside, John got the left leg, I got the right, and we hauled back on the deer until the antlers scraped the bumper and the bulk of the deer reached the tipping point. He fell in the trunk on top of us. We were both a mess – covered in mud and blood – but at least the deer was loaded.

Once out of the trunk, we took a long look at John's kill lying there in the lantern's glow. I was so proud of my son's accomplishment. The smile on my twelve-year-old's face was worth everything.

I said "Let's get him over to Lancaster's. We need to get there before they fill up the cooler."

After a few more moments admiring the kill, we backed out of the swamp road and turned into Lancaster's Deer Processing shed fifteen minutes later.

I pulled the car up the gravel drive at Lancaster's, put it in reverse, and backed slowly toward the skinning hoist as several small groups of hunters moved aside. Every observer, I am sure, had his own thoughts about these obvious newcomers, in a car, no less. I stopped just short of the skinning rack. John piled out on his side as I popped the lid of the trunk.

Several small does and a young four-point buck already lay on the ground ready to be cleaned. A decent-size buck – a two-year-old six-point – already hung on the hoist.

Still in my muddy business clothes, including my yellow pajama top that I had completely forgotten about, I joined my son. The curious group of seasoned camouflaged hunters all gathered to see what in the world was in the trunk of my car.

John's four-year-old buck was undisputedly the best kill that had been brought in that week. Getting the deer out of the trunk was no trouble. All the other hunters pitched in and helped. Weighing the buck on the scales was now top priority for us and those seasoned hunters. The needle on the big brass spring scales settled at one-ninety. All the older men congratulated John. They knew a real wall hanger when they saw it.

Some patted him on the back. Others said, "Nice deer, son." and others "Great job, young man."

Craig Lancaster, owner of the skinning shed, told John, "I clean a lot of deer in a season. Not many grown men kill a buck that big."

I was one proud dad!

When we finally reached home, I slipped into the bedroom and phoned Craig. I told him to please cape out John's trophy buck and I would have it mounted as a surprise.

I thought, *What a great Christmas present – my twelve-year-old bow hunter's first deer.*

A BUCK NINETY-FIVE

The much-used Browning bow was settled in my lap, arrow notched, release tight on my wrist. I was eighteen feet up in a fifty-year-old red oak sitting on a two-by-four I had nailed across two sprawling branches. The board wasn't that comfortable, but the crude wooden stand overlooked a productive, natural funnel created by a small duck pond and the base of a steep ridge covered in tall, mature white oaks.

This was my most favorite deer stand on our small, Union county farm. As I settled in and determined to remain still, the thought of the buck I had seen from this very perch on Saturday gave me enough motivation to sit motionless for a month. He was big. Really big. In fact, he was the biggest deer I would ever see in this part of the South Carolina Upcountry.

And now, thirty-six years later, I can tell you I never saw him again. But that old boy showed me a secret, one I have never told to a soul.

That mid-October morning in 1981 I was sitting in my stand, long before light on the woodland floor was a thought. As the first harsh shafts of eastern gold pierced the fall forest, a light breeze whispered, precipitating a wonderworld. Leaves, by the score, flittered down and across the ridge. Scarlet-tipped dogwoods, saffron hickories, cinnamon oaks, and orange sweet gum leaves created a curtain of color as they danced through the sunlight. If you have not experienced such a moment, it would be difficult to convince you of its unmatched beauty.

And then a rain began. Plop-plop plop-plop. No, not big drops of water, but apple-green acorns. By the scores, they escaped their knurled brown caps. It was as if a dinner bell was calling out. Squirrels, turkeys, and deer appeared.

I had never heard anything like it.

The acorns fell fast and hard. They hit the limbs of trees before landing on the leafy, forest floor. They fell into the small pond behind me. They struck the steps of my stand and even bounced off my compound bow, creating a metallic binging noise that made me wince. This extraordinary show by Mother Nature mesmerized me.

As so often happens, he was just there, appearing out of nowhere. The largest buck I had ever seen was ghosting along, sixty yards up the ridge, rapidly gorging on every acorn he heard fall.

I froze, moving only my eyes with heart thundering, I prayed he might work his way close enough. I pledged in my heart I would not even draw on such a magnificent creature unless he came within twenty yards of me and I had a broadside shot. One lifetime would not be long enough to regret a crippling shot on such a trophy. The buck was feeding fast, as if he had found the mother lode. He was not going to share a single morsel. He moved a little closer, I watched and prayed. Prayed and watched. I tried to control my breathing.

As the minutes slipped by, he continued to feed. I noticed something that I had never paid attention to before. Every time an acorn fell, the old rascal would glance up, note where it hit, and move in that direction. Every sound seemed to lure him a step or two toward that distinctive plop on the leaves or toward the thop of the acorn hitting a limb on its tumble to the ground. Forty yards out, he slowly but steadily approached.

Just as I was easing my way up into a standing position, a bachelor group of old Tom turkeys, five full grown ones in all, slipped in from my left. With equal fervor they, too, began gobbling up the green nuggets.

With five pairs of the best eyes in the business not twenty-feet from me, I dared not blink. I was pinned down for the next ten minutes as the turkeys fed back up the ridge. The deer was still browsing, slowly making its way down the ridge. It looked like a shot might still work out when there, below my stand, a large bobcat that had made it undetected to the base of my big oak darted in toward the nearest turkey. They, as one, exploded into the air. The force from their powerful wing beats almost blew my cap off.

The deer whirled by instinct and vanished into the hardwoods. In ten seconds I was alone. It was stone, graveyard, dead silent.

It took me another hour of just sitting there to realize nothing was coming back; no deer, no turkeys, and no bobcat. My dream deer was gone. I replayed that scene over and over in my mind all day Sunday. Oh, how I wished it wasn't Sunday. As a child I was never allowed to hunt on Sunday. We were brought up that Sunday was a holy day, a day we were to be in church both morning and evening. That childhood rule stuck through my adult life, too. My return to the woods would just have to wait until Monday.

Sunday night I called my backup at work, and we agreed to trade off a couple hours Monday morning. It's good to have at least some non-hunting friends.

At 1:00 A.M. Monday morning I saw my trophy deer for the second time in forty-two hours. He was even bigger than I thought the first time I saw him. A state record to be sure. I had parked the twelve-year-old 4x4 truck just inside the gate. I changed into my scent-free coveralls I keep in a separate bag and then rubber knee-length boots. Camouflage cotton gloves with the fingertips worn out, face mask, and a short bill cap completed the preparations.

It was a good three-quarters of a mile to the old stand tree, so I left in plenty of time. It was pitch-dark, but the sandy farm road guided me silently almost to the woods. I dared not use a flashlight and almost ran into the barbed wire fence twenty yards from the wood line. I lay down, slid the bow and quiver through, and rolled under the tight bottom strand. Now, one extra careful step at a time, I made it through the oaks and into the stand in a tad over thirty minutes. Daybreak came slowly. The trees turned from black, to charcoal, and then light gray. The old bruiser came with first light. He fed on the big green acorns down the ridge to a perfect twenty-yard broadside shot. I took my time. I controlled my breathing. He looked as big as a Colorado elk, but I was determined not to get buck fever. I slowly – ever so slowly – drew to full draw. Locked my thumb behind my neck, bowstring just kissing my cheek, put the twenty-yard pin one inch above his massive shoulders and squeezed the trigger to my release. At that instant the bow-string parted with a loud crack and I bolted straight up in bed. It scared my wife too, who jolted awake saying, "What's wrong, you okay?"

I looked over at the alarm clock. 3:15 A.M. "Just a terrible nightmare. It's okay. Go back to sleep."

She did. I didn't.

Monday dawned as a repeat of Saturday. My hopes were high as I hauled my bow up to my tree stand using a twenty-five-foot length of braided green decoy anchor cord. No post-dawn breeze, however, created the mosaic of colors of Saturday. Within thirty minutes I realized something else about the day was different. Very different. No acorns. None were falling, not one. The silence was unnerving.

I tried to console myself that the lack of falling acorns would not matter. The acorns had probably already fallen on the ground, and the deer would return no doubt. But nothing happened. The woods remained unusually quiet. I sat still as a post for two hours, seeing no turkeys and no monster deer. In fact, not even a doe with a three-month-old fawn crossed my path. I was fixing to un-notch my arrow and ease my bow down when I glimpsed movement on the ridge - just a glint of sunlight off an unfamiliar object. I was scared to even blink my eyes as I might lose sight of the brief reflection. The glint moved exposing one piece of an antler. A flicker several feet further back was the unmistakable swish of a short brown-and-white tail.

My heart seemed to skip beats.

For the next few minutes I caught sight of just bits and pieces of the deer. I knew it was a buck, but was it *my* buck? I lost sight of him entirely for ten minutes but then caught a good side view. It wasn't old big boy from Saturday, but it was an impressive three-to-four-year-old. Maybe a borderline shot if hunting with my .270, but this deer was definitely a shooter for me with my bow. The buck, though, was not feeding in my direction. He was just drifting right-to-left, sixty yards out, nibbling on the odd acorn.

I knew if the deer continued in the direction he was headed, I could forget about a shot. It was then I remembered the deer's behavior I had witnessed on Saturday. It was the sound. The sound of the acorns hitting the ground that guided the big deer. Expecting the acorns to still be dropping, I had not thought of bringing a pocket of small rocks or some other object that could imitate that distinctive sound.

When the deer melted behind another big white oak I inched my way to a standing position and ever so slowly slid my hand into my left pocket. My fingertips touched a few coins, so I gathered them, and watching the deer closely, eased my hand out of my camouflage pants pocket. Slowly I opened my hand revealing five coins.

I have never been keen on throwing money away, but I knew I had nothing else. Why not give it a try? I waited for the deer to lower his head, and flipped a dime out about five feet in front of my stand. It hit the leaves with a respectable plop. I studied the deer's reaction. Just like on Saturday, the deer stopped feeding and jerked his head toward the direction of the noise. He put his head back down and picked up another acorn. I held my breath.

The next step he took was in the direction of my hiding place. I then waited five, maybe ten, minutes without moving a muscle. The deer, a good sixty-five yards out, was now facing my stand. Waiting until he lowered his head again, I flipped a nickel in the same general direction as the dime. The nickel hit the ground with a little more oomph. Again the deer lifted his head and took several steps in my direction.

A second nickel and then a quarter got the buck about forty yards off my left shoulder. Unhurriedly he fed along and gradually closed the gap.

It was now critical that I not make any false move. I had only one coin left – a Liberty half-dollar. Needing to raise my bow into position and be ready to draw, I held the shiny coin in my left hand. Slowly – ever so slowly – I transferred it to between the thumb and forefinger of my right hand. My release tightly fitted to my right wrist was ready and locked onto the bowstring. I would only need my forefinger after I drew the arrow back to make the shot. I got the bow up.

The tension of this moment was almost unbearable. Five more yards and a slight turn would set up the shot. My heart was thumping so loudly it sounded like a tom-tom, my hands were sweaty, and my knees began to tremble a little from the awkward position and the adrenaline rush. It was now or never. I opened my thumb and forefinger and let the Liberty fall.

Striking the first step of my stand, the coin sounded like a bomb in the deafening silence of the moment. The coin then bounced, hit a lower limb of the oak and ricocheted out in front of the stand to my left, a good fifteen feet.

I was doomed! It was all over – I expected the deer to whirl and be out of sight in a flash. But to my surprise, a squirrel foraging at the base of the oak and unseen until now, darted toward the half-dollar. The greedy buck, not to be robbed, bounded to the spot in two easy leaps and landed in front of me.

I came to full draw using the commotion as cover and I let the arrow fly. As if in slow motion, the bright yellow-and-green fletching disappeared into his muscular shoulder and reappeared as it buried itself in the leaf-covered ground. The buck leapt and bounded twenty yards before his front legs gave out, causing him to slide to a stop on his side. I was shaking so badly I had to just sit awhile. I finally climbed down, rested the bow against the oak and walked over to the deer. As I knelt by the deer, my legs felt like jelly, my heartbeat was throbbing in my ears, and I was breathing so hard you would have thought I had run a mile. The beautiful eight-pointer had a symmetrical rack, good mass, and

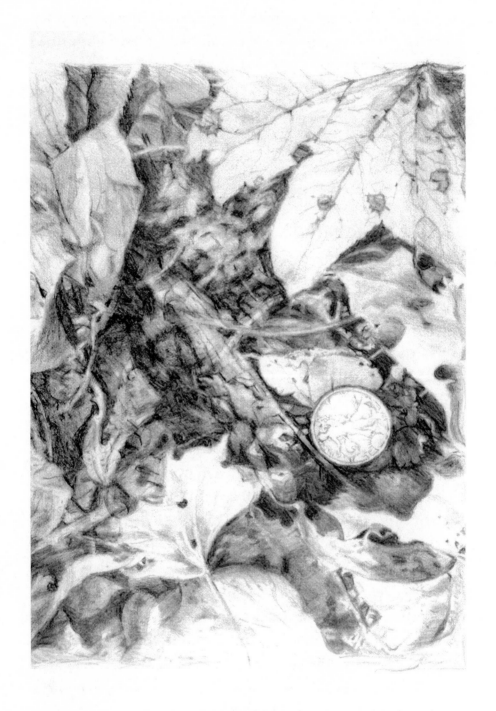

tall tangs. I slid my hand down his side and stroked him on his strong shoulder.

He was a beauty. What a trophy!

As I went back to the oak to pick up my bow I spied the half-dollar among the leaves. Picking it up, I noticed the other coins gleaming in the late morning sunlight. I gathered all of them, spread my hand, and mentally calculated - one dime, two nickels, a single quarter, and the half-dollar. Ninety-five cents.

I jingled the change in my hand and I thought, *A buck ninety-five*.

CAKE AND ICE CREAM

You have probably heard many times the old wives' tale that right before you die a tragic, unexpected death, your whole life passes before you. Let me tell you, this is not true. You are too busy trying to figure out how to save yourself to be watching a black-and-white video in your head.

I will tell you how I know.

In 1978 Claudia and I took every dime we had, mortgaged all but our two young children, and bought a business in Spartanburg, South Carolina. Shortly after I moved here and got my family settled in, I met Kirk Neely who was my same age. His family, which included four sons, put my son John and me on a path of raising our boys together through sports, church activities, and Boy Scouts. After many years of camping trips, hikes, summer camps, and working on merit badge requirements together, all earned their Eagle Scout awards. Through these years of activities together, Kirk and I became best friends.

Best of all, Kirk was an avid fisherman. When family time would permit, one of us would put together a fishing trip.

Most of these trips were to local farm ponds fishing for largemouth bass and bream. One Saturday, however, we decided to explore the fishing possibilities at Lake Jocassee near Salem, North Carolina. We had heard a lot about folks catching big lake trout up there in this 7500 acre, 365-foot-deep lake. The lake was formed when Duke Power Company dammed up the Toxaway, Horsepasture, Thompson, and Whitewater Rivers.

Actually, Duke Power had built two lakes by damming up Bad Creek and Western Bad Creek. The Bad Creek Project, as it was called, was designed to generate power in a unique way. Lake Jocassee was 1200 feet below the Bad Creek Reservoir. The two were connected by over a mile of massive tunnels carved through solid granite. As is normal with hydroelectric projects, when demand for energy was highest, the water from Bad Creek would flow down the tunnels through four generators at Jocassee pump station and produce electricity. The unique feature of this project, however, was that when demand for energy was low, usually late at night, huge pumps would suck water out of Jocassee and pump the water through the tunnel and back up the 1200 feet to Bad Creek Reservoir. The suction created by these enormous pumps was notorious.

On a crisp late fall Saturday morning in 1983, Kirk and I left out for Lake Jocassee, driving up Highway 11 through some of the most beautiful country in the state. All the way up you had views of the Blue Ridge Mountains. After an hour we turned right onto Jocassee Road and pulled up to Hoyett's Grocery & Tackle, last stop before the road dead-ended into the put-in ramps of the lake.

In the early '80s there were still real country stores. These institutions guarded every rural crossroad and lake landing. Hoyett's was typical. Every man working pulpwood or construction in the area knew of this spot. You would sit on a weathered picnic table at lunch and enjoy a healthy slab of aged hand-cut hoop cheese. You could choose Bluebird Vienna sausage or potted meat in a can. A sleeve of Premium Saltine crackers and a tin of sardines was also a popular choice. It was essential to pick out a can of sardines with the key that opened the tin top still attached to the lid. Otherwise, a pocket knife was required.

For fishermen gas, motor oil, live shad for bait, Lance Peanut Butter and Cheese Snack Crackers, beer, soft drinks, and ice might top the list. But what fisherman, even with a full tackle box, could escape Hoyett's without cruising the crowded aisles? Assorted lures like Deep-R-Doodle, River Runt, Wee Louie, Super Spook, and Waddle Bugs in colorfully decorated die-cut boxes would demand that they be added to an ever-growing collection.

Kirk and I arrived at the store at ten that morning, snack time. We had planned an exploratory trip and had not even brought our rods. We were fishing for information. We would not act too anxious. A little disinterested. We would get our usual Moon Pie and RC Cola and just stroll through the store. About midway through the cola, we planned to approach the counter and engage the owner in conversation. Ask casual questions, not seeming overly interested in the answers.

"How's the fishing been?"

"Any big ones caught lately?"

"See you carry live shad. That what most folks using?"

On cue, one of us would stroll over to a wall near the door that was full of pictures held by rusty staples – happy men, women, or children were holding quite large trout.

While looking at the pictures we would ask, "Most of these caught at night?"

"What's your peak fishing month up here?"

It was not the first time either party had played the game. I felt a little sorry for the store owner during this song and dance routine. Being the ultimate salesman, the store proprietor would be caught between ensuring your ultimate return to fish and telling the absolute truth. But in the end, that old saying "a picture is worth a thousand words" and the ones on the wall sealed the deal.

We would be back.

Since Kirk is a native of Spartanburg who knows everybody, we decided, on the way back home, that he would ask around about someone taking us fishing on Lake Jocassee. Two months into his inquiries Kirk found Beaver Burgess, a local fellow who was a part-time guide. He specialized in night trips up on the lake. Our first trip with Beaver on February 10, 1984, was on a night so cold the mercury was at the bottom of the tube and we had to constantly break the ice off the ferrule of our spinning rods.

The entire time we were helping launch Beaver's pontoon boat, he kept saying, "The colder it gets, the better the big trout bite." I figured we were going to need an additional eighty-quart cooler to bring our fish home. It was that cold. Beaver's pontoon had been customized for this subfreezing midnight madness. He could pull heavy canvas curtains around the pontoon's top, and he had attached to the boat's floor an honest-to-goodness four-foot-tall kerosene stove to beat back the cold.

On these nocturnal adventures the pattern went like this. We would meet Beaver at Hoyett's store about dusk dark, gas the pontoon, and supplement the supper we had put up at home with extra candy bars, Slim Jim jerky sticks, and packages of fried pork skins. We would launch the boat right at twilight and motor to the Round House Point, Beaver's preferred fishing spot.

After testing the wind, Beaver would anchor the boat with a preposterously long three-quarter-inch braided rope, draw the heavy curtains on the three sides upwind, and hang a large electric light over the open side. Within minutes, scads of bait fish would school in the penetrating cone of white light aimed at the water, which was gin-clear. The balance of preparation consisted of baiting hooks with a frisky live shad, feeding out the number of pulls on the line that Beaver would somehow divine, firing up the stove, and putting on a pot of coffee. All tasks completed, we often began a twelve-hour marathon of telling as many fishing stories as three people could think of – some true, but most, vast exaggerations. The stories we told on these trips bring to mind a quote from William Fox, "Of all the liars among mankind, the fisherman is the most trustworthy."

We followed this routine for several Friday nights through the winter of '84, with some, but not fantastic, success. We would catch nice trout in the two-to three-pound size, but not one of us landed a single strike of a really big fish.

Following a night of fishing, we stopped at Hoyett's store for a sunup cup of coffee before heading back home and admired an expensive pontoon rig at the gas pump. When we were at the counter paying up, Jimmy Orr, the owner, who knew us pretty well by now, said casually, "You fellows ought to try Travis. That's his boat out there. He's been experimenting with trolling downriggers and is catching some really nice lake trout."

We wasted no time introducing ourselves to Travis. Before we left, we had scheduled a trip and happily drove home. Over the next few trips out with Travis we caught some pretty fish. We liked Travis a lot. He was a nice enough fellow, a good guide, and, best of all, the trips were in warm weather.

Travis was one of those guides who was always trying new things, experimenting with new techniques and lures. For me that has always been a characteristic of a better than average guide. On one of our trips with Travis he shared with us his thought about needing a metal attractor to run before his deep-rigged spoon. It had to be ultra-thin, big and flashy. He could not find metal that had that combination of features.

I, however, had just the ticket. Our metal fabricating business uses very thin brass to shim large pumps to the precise height of the motors that drive them. I made Travis several samples, which he began using. Soon all three of us were developing a close friendship. Not only were Kirk and I good, paying customers, but we were also helping Travis develop a new style of trolling.

Kirk and I were having such a good time on these trips with Travis that I got the bright idea to invite our two Dads to go fishing as their birthday present. We envisioned a grand occasion, going out a little early, pulling up to a sandbar, having a leisurely cookout, and then fishing through the warm summer evening. What an absolutely perfect gift for our fathers! We set the date. I made all the arrangements with Travis and instructed him not to worry about the cost of some really good steaks and all the fixings.

When the appointed day came, we four arrived a little early on a beautiful summer afternoon. There was not a cloud in the sky. It was shirtsleeve weather. What a great evening! We were all very excited.

Right on time Travis' red Ford pickup and pontoon came over the rise of the parking area and boat landing. Travis stopped a little ways off - something I thought strange - got out, and came over to meet our dads.

Just after introductions had been made and Travis had shaken hands with everyone, a second pickup and pontoon pulled up to the spot where we were standing. As the fellow got out, Travis looked over his shoulder, motioned this stranger over, and turning to us said, "This is Leon. He's going to be your guide tonight."

Stunned, I cut my eyes over to Kirk who just raised both eyebrows in a "What's the deal?" expression. As Travis, with great fanfare, began introducing Leon to everyone, I glanced over at Leon's boat, seeing immediately that it had not the slightest resemblance to the nice pontoon Travis owned. Leon's rig - if in fact it was Leon's - was rough. It had no top, no center console, and no steering wheel. The outboard engine for a boat of its type and size, I judged to be grossly underpowered. The engine's long tiller dictated that the operator stand at the rear of the boat to steer the motor. The entire rig, very antiquated, looked like it would float, but I was more than a little skeptical about this whole situation.

As Travis finished up the introductions, I heard him mumble, "I can't go." He quickly steered our group down to the dock where Leon was launching his boat. It is strange, but these things can sometimes get a momentum of their own. We loaded all the gear, coolers, rods, tackle boxes, and bags of groceries.

Leon's motor started on the first pull of the starter cord, which caused me to relax a tad. We pulled away from the dock. Just before we rounded the point, I glanced back to the parking area and saw Travis and four other customers loading out for a night of fishing on Travis' boat. Now I knew. Travis had double booked the trips and we had been sold out. I had only one other guide pull this trick on me one other time, and I knew then I would never fish with Travis again. Not wanting to break up the party, I did not say anything to the others. I just hoped for the best.

We cruised along the steep, heavily wooded shoreline as the sun offered a real light show over the mountains. The western sky was on fire. The lake was calm, but reflected the sky's riot of color. The evening was absolutely beautiful and the temperature perfect. After an hour, Leon nosed the bow of the boat onto a picture-perfect sandy island. The lightning bugs shared their glow as the bats jabbed through the dusk. That old seaman's saying, "Red at night, sailors delight, red in the morning, sailors take warning," came to my mind. Maybe it was a good omen. I tried to relax.

The sheer granite walls of the shore were so steep in places we could cruise along and almost touch the rock. The scenery was very dramatic. We could peer into the clear jade-green water and see twenty feet down. It was difficult to comprehend just how deep Jocassee was. Waterfalls like the Laurel Fall, Mills Creek, and Wright Creek cascade directly into the lake.

Leon began unloading the items he needed to cook supper. He had brought an impressive hand-forged outdoor grill and he expertly built a fire in minutes. Whatever Leon might not be, he was without a doubt a very accomplished camp cook. Leon put on a nice supper. The steaks were cooked to perfection.

Everyone was enjoying themselves with good food and fellowship. Stories that began, "Remember that time ..." were entertaining everyone. I began to relax a little more.

Maybe this is going to turn out okay after all, I thought. We had all night to fish, so everyone was just taking their time.

Leon's cooking rig included a metal arm that supported a two-quart enamel coffee pot. As the lake water in the pot came to a boil, Leon threw in a double handful of fresh coffee. It smelled wonderful. After a few minutes he removed the pot from the fire and poured in a cup of cold lake water which carried all the grounds to the bottom of the pot – an old cowboy trick I had witnessed before. We enjoyed some of the best coffee I had ever had. Anything cooked out over an open fire always tastes great!

Full as ticks, we loaded our gear back on the boat and started down the lake in a direction Kirk and I had never traveled before with either Beaver or Travis. Somewhat puzzled I asked, "Leon, where are we headed?"

Over the engine noise, the reply was, "To the dam."

A half-hour run later we began to see the outline of two gargantuan concrete and steel towers. They were silhouetted by the harsh bluish-white lights that illuminated the towers, catwalks, dam, and water for a hundred feet in every direction, I knew instantly these towers held the giant intakes that pumped the water back up to Bad Creek.

Because of my business, I had heard a lot about this project and particularly about the tunnels that connect the two lakes. One of our customers had obtained a contract during the construction of these tunnels to furnish and service Porta Potties throughout this network of tunnels. We had built him a tandem axle truck with a four- thousand-gallon water tank mounted on it. Each day the operator would drive throughout these tunnels and flush out the Porta Potties. On occasion this customer would show us pictures of these impressive tunnels that dwarfed even his big tank truck. Looking at those pictures made me think it would be difficult to imagine the volume of water flowing back and forth between the lakes.

The sight of those towers we were approaching just reinforced in my mind the massiveness of the structure and the power of this water.

About that time I realized we must turn quickly to avoid hitting a 4 foot x 8 foot sign suspended from a long cable over the water. In the eerie glow of the reflected light the sign read,

This sign and its cable created a sizable barrier, certainly nothing temporary. Just then, Leon also saw the cable. He quickly veered left, just missing the sign.

Confused, I jerked around and asked, "Are we going to go under the cable?"

"Oh yeah," Leon said. "That's just for people who don't fish up here very much. The sign don't really mean nothing. We won't have no problems."

Sliding right under the cable and heading toward the dam, Leon steered the boat right up to the bank. He handed me the short bow line and asked me to jump out. "You hold this, and I'll be right back," Leon instructed.

Opening a storage area in the pontoon, Leon pulled out a long yellow ski rope – nothing particularly impressive, just a regular plastic ski rope. He then ran up the bank, letting out rope all the way. At the end of the catwalk that led out to the nearest pump tower, Leon started out, got pretty close to the midway point between the bank and the tower, then tied that end of the rope to the catwalk. He came back and brought the other end of the rope down, hopped on the boat, and pushed it away from the dam. After pulling the boat so that we were pretty much directly under the catwalk, he tied the boat up to an aluminum loop welded to the bow of the boat with almost no slack in the rope. Now we were tied up and in almost complete darkness – except for the glow from the bluish-white security lights that was reflected on the mirror smooth surface of the lake.

For a few seconds no one said anything. It was stone, grave-yard, dead quiet. We just stood there in the shadow of this loom-ing steel and concrete structure. Finally Dad said, "Well, let's get to it," and we broke out the fishing stuff and baited up.

Not five minutes had passed when a girl, maybe eight or nine, and her grandfather drove up on the edge of the dam, got out of their pickup, and walked out on the catwalk all the way to the tower. Carrying a metal minnow bucket and two rods, they obviously knew exactly what they were doing. In short order they began catching good-sized trout. Seeing these hefty trout being reeled up almost directly in front of our faces created a lot of excitement on our boat. Again I felt that maybe everything was going to work out fine.

Within twenty minutes however, my sense of calm was shat-tered when a loud monotone voice, obviously a recording, boomed over a speaker, "This is the control tower. The pumps will start in five minutes. Clear the area. I repeat, clear the area. The pumps will start in five minutes."

I turned around and asked Leon, "What does that mean?"

DANGER
WATER INTAKE
STAY CLEAR

Dad said, "I think it means what it said. Clear out."

The grandfather and little girl reeled in immediately, picked up their stringer of trout and bait bucket, and started off the catwalk.

Big Kirk said, "Yeah, I think that's our cue. Let's fish another spot. It's a big lake."

"It won't be no problem. Don't worry about that," Leon said.

I was worrying!

I thought, *Man, I don't know about this.*

It was very strange, and nothing Leon said or did was making good sense. Red flags were going up all over the place. Well, in five minutes on the dot, those pumps cranked up with a roar, drowning out all other sounds and sending vibrations through the water, boat, and even into my legs.

Almost instantly water was pulled through the intakes of the tower. Within seconds the level of the lake between the boat and those towers was actually dropping! When you first say that to somebody, they'll say water always seeks its level and that part of the lake could not be lower. Well, the water in a bathtub or toilet near the drain is substantially lower than the water on the outside edge of the vortex. On a very large scale, that is exactly what began to happen to Lake Jocassee that night and we were right in the middle of it!

A vortex began to develop around the towers as the water was being pulled down. It grew and began pulling the pontoon closer and closer to its edge. The only thing keeping the boat from sliding into what was beginning to be a very deep, ominous hole was that small ski rope. The length was just enough to keep us from swinging next to the tower, but the vortex was growing by the second, becoming wider, deeper, and more powerful.

The suddenness and magnitude of our problem immobilized us. In the pitch dark in the shadow of the tower, the five of us peered into this growing hole that was swallowing everything. We were just hanging on the edge. At that moment I remembered a bit of proverbial wisdom old folks used when a friend or loved one was about to die, "He's just circling the drain." It became completely clear in my mind that if we got any further into the vortex, we were absolutely going to die. Nothing would keep us from getting sucked down into that abyss and drowning. Quite frankly, I was terrified.

I kept looking over my shoulder into the hole, then back and forth toward Leon to gauge his reaction. He was petrified. Kirk, like me, saw the seriousness of our situation and had quickly determined our guide was useless. Kirk was already rushing to take control of the motor. He started the motor, shifted into reverse, put it over as far as he could to the port side, and was trying to back the boat away. I moved to the front of the boat where the rope was tied. The problem was that the rope was keeping us from pulling away from the danger just as much as it was from keeping the boat from disappearing into the vortex. It was obvious that the outboard motor was not powerful enough to overcome the suction of the towers. We were hanging in limbo as we were ever so slowly being pulled closer and closer to the vortex. The suction wasn't critical yet, but closer to the center, it picked up speed and power.

Now, with Kirk in the rear working the motor, and me up in the front, I realized the rope was actually keeping us from pulling away from this vortex. When I hollered to Kirk, "I'm going to untie this rope," the guide went a little crazy.

He screamed, "No, don't cut the rope! Don't cut the rope! We'll go into the hole. Don't cut the rope!"

I had no idea whether the boat's motor was actually strong enough to pull us away from the towers. The rope had tremendous pressure on it. The water level was actually dropping, and the rope had grown ever tighter against the front of the pontoon. A substantial crack started developing in a weld seam on the front of the starboard pontoon. The rope was trying to hold up that whole side of the pontoon. I was convinced I had no other choice.

I hollered back to Kirk, "The boat is coming apart! When I cut the rope, give the engine all the power you've got. Go straight back so it is not pulling us on an angle. Steer us directly away from that vortex."

During the entire conversation, Leon was screaming with panic, "Don't do it! Don't do it!"

It should have been obvious to him that without trying something, we were all going to die right there on the spot. The boat was getting ready to come completely apart.

I started sawing on the rope with my pocket knife. Halfway through, the pressure snapped the rope with a crack. Kirk pushed the tiller dead center, giving the motor all the throttle he could muster. Slowly this new angle made a difference and the back of the boat pulled away from the tower towards the safety of dry land.

When we finally reached the dam, it was as if only then did everybody remember to breathe. Somewhat stunned and without a word, our two dads began to untangle the fishing equipment. Kirk and I began to straighten up the rest of the gear that was in a mess. Leon, however, just sat there on the floor, knees pulled up to his chest with arms locked around his legs, just rocking back and forth, not saying or doing anything.

The four of us were done! We had lost all interest in fishing. Once the boat was tidied up, Kirk headed us to the landing. After ducking back under the warning cable, Kirk steered by the distant light of the parking area.

As we started back across the lake, I kept a sharp eye on the pontoon to be sure it was going to hold together.

It was quiet now; just the purr of the engine as we steered toward the landing. Leon seemed to be in shock. He had not uttered a word since we started for the dock. Throughout the entire trip back, he remained seated on the floor, arms locked tightly around his knees.

Dad finally broke the silence, "Man that was a close call. For two years I was on an aircraft carrier fighting kamikaze pilots all the way across the Pacific and I was never that scared."

No one else said anything, but all of us were silently feeling the same. I don't think anyone on the boat ever had been that frightened before. Certainly not me.

Once we docked, I tied up the boat. Unable to get Leon to move, we loaded his gear in the back of his pickup and tucked the money for the trip over the sun visor.

As we pulled out of the parking lot, Mr. Neely, Big Kirk as everyone called him, laughed, "What a birthday! Next time let's just do cake and ice cream!"

NOBODY WILL BELIEVE IT!

I lost my cell phone. I had not had it long.

My wife, who is in charge of communications in our company, and our son, John III, had decided I needed to upgrade to one of the new iPhones.

I was completely happy with my old flip phone and suspected this new concern that I have one of the latest and greatest technological marvels had something to do with their theory that if I had a new phone then logically they too would need one. So I had a new phone. And now it was gone.

For two days I quietly looked for my new phone. I did not want to admit I had lost it. I had pitched a hissy fit when I found out what the thing cost. And now it was gone.

I had searched high and low. I had even driven back down to our small farm near Jonesville. There I had spent most of the previous Saturday. I was showing my good friend, Todd Stott, where I wanted him to put up some new barbed wire fencing.

I had retraced my steps carefully over all the places Todd and I had been that day. Still no luck.

On Monday I finally owned up to my wife that my phone was gone and I had absolutely no idea where it was. This was very hard for me to do. It only confirmed in her mind that I truly am one of the most forgetful people she knows. We had a difference of opinion on this matter, but the present situation like the phone being missing weakens my case considerably. After eating a hearty portion of humble pie, I asked did she think we should order another one. I should not have asked that question as it seemed to upset her a great deal. Her parting remark was, "You better find that phone!"

As a final desperate effort I shared my plight with John III, who, at thirty-four years old, was our in-resident Information Technology expert. I went to his office late Monday and bared my soul. I had lost my new phone and his mother was not happy. Without looking up from the computer he was busy typing into, he said, "No problem."

"It is a problem," I said. "She's really upset. I've looked everywhere for the phone, and it is nowhere to be found."

"No problem, I think I can help you find it," John said. "We'll go look for it tomorrow morning before work. I'll meet you here at 7:00 A.M."

This was the best news I had heard in two days. I went home and at supper announced to Claudia, my wife, "John says not to worry, he can find the phone. We are going to get it before work in the morning." I decided a positive tone might help in this situation.

John was right on time. He had his laptop computer with him. As I drove down Highway 176 he said, "Now we need to retrace where you drove or walked on Saturday."

He began explaining that my new phone had a feature he termed Find My iPhone and that he had turned this app on so he could see on his laptop screen where the phone was. In this early version of the iPhone apparently this feature was very general in nature. The area the phone was in was quite large the further you were away from it, and it got smaller the closer you were to the missing phone. I glanced over at his computer screen as I drove down 176 and could see a large light-green circle on the map. It was, I estimated, fifteen miles in diameter.

John asked, "What road did you take to the farm and back on Saturday?"

I told him, "I went down Highway 176 to the Kangaroo Express convenience store and met Todd Stott, my fence man."

"Okay," John said, "we'll stop at the convenience store first. Did you have your phone when you stopped at the convenience store?"

"Yes, for sure, because I called him to let him know I would be driving my olive- green truck. I know I had it then, but I don't know if I had it when I left. It's possible I dropped it or left it on the roof of the truck. I looked for it Sunday, but I didn't find it near where I had parked at the store when Todd and I met and talked."

"Alright," John said, "when we get there we'll see if it might have been found and turned in to the store clerk."

We pulled up in the acre-size parking lot and John said, "You stay out here in the grassy area next to where you two talked and I'll go into the store. When I get inside I'm going to make the alarm on the phone ring."

"You can make it do that?" I asked, surprised.

"Yes, but we don't know how long the phone has been on, or what condition the battery is in. I don't want to let it ring but a few times so we won't use up the battery. Listen for it out here, and I'll take the computer into the store and set off the alarm. If someone found it and turned it in, I will be able to hear the alarm ring even if it's in a drawer."

John went through the double glass doors and I waited. Five minutes later he came out and I said, "Nothing out here. What about inside?"

"Not there and the clerk said no one had turned one in."

We loaded up and headed down West Spring Road on the final leg to the farm.

I said to my son, "John, when we get to the farm I think we should go straight to the barn. I'll get the John Deere Gator and drive us over all the areas I drove Saturday when Todd and I discussed the fence work."

John, eyes always watching the laptop's screen, agreed that was a good idea. We turned in to the farm property and stopped at the galvanized gate.

John said, "Dad the phone is here at the farm. The search area tightened up quite a bit just as we turned in."

This made me feel a lot better, but I was still not convinced this new high-tech approach was going to find my phone and get me out of hot water with my wife. As we drove the quarter-mile dirt road toward the barn to get my four-wheel drive Gator, we neared the narrow crossing of the right-of-way where the power line runs through the woods to the barn and our log cabin.

John, with excitement in his voice, said, "Dad, quick, stop here! The search area just dropped again in size. I think we're pretty close."

I stopped the truck and we piled out.

"Dad, did you drive the Gator up the power line on Saturday or stay on the dirt road when you and Mr. Stott went to look at the fence?" John asked.

I thought a second. "We came up the power line. I asked Todd if he minded if I stopped on the right-of-way to exchange the flash card in the trail camera that is right at the head of the food plot. He and I both got out right down there a bit, maybe fifty yards."

I told Todd we had planted a number of small plots of clover and purple-top turnips as protein-rich food for the deer and turkeys. The motion-activated cameras are a fine way to record just what wildlife variety is using these areas. It was one of these cameras I checked on Saturday with Todd.

John said, "Good. I think we should set off the alarm here and just take our chances that the battery will hold up. Listen close. Here goes."

John typed some code into the computer. A couple of seconds passed. Then we both heard the alarm loud and clear. The sound was coming from right where a much-used deer trail crosses the power line. Leading to the food plot, I keep a trail camera on at all times. It was this camera I changed out the flash card in on Saturday.

John and I turned to each other and grinned. Bingo! We had found my phone! Just then our attention was drawn back to the power line by a huge ruckus. We were in time to see a very nice eight-point buck, frightened by this new, unusual, and loud alarm, as he burst out of some thick wild plum bushes that bordered the power line. He had bedded down in the sunshine not ten feet from where the lost phone lay ringing. This deer was a real shooter. Old timers call a big buck like this a rooster deer. I knew this buck well. I had seen him on my trail camera off and on for over two years, but had never gotten a shot at him. Being that close when this old boy tore across the power line today solidified my resolve that I needed to hunt this buck and hunt him hard.

John and I both were very distracted by the size and commotion the deer made and temporarily forgot all about the phone which was continuing to sound a steady, shrill alarm.

After the predictable exclamations:

"Dad, did you see the size of that buck?!"

"Man, was that some deer?! Could you believe he was bedded down right there on the open power line?!" I said. "Todd and I must have passed within ten yards of him Saturday and that old rascal just held tight."

We waited a couple minutes more, then John and I walked the short distance down the power line toward the alarm and there in the foot-tall Byhalia grass was my phone. The slim black phone was turned on its edge and held by the thick grass. In this position it was almost undetectable. We would never have found it without the alarm. I was impressed.

I was very glad to have my phone back. Very glad. But my enthusiasm for finding the phone was completely overshadowed. I had an eyewitness account that the best buck on the farm was bedding down not fifty yards from our food plot and one of my favorite ladder stand locations.

John and I gathered up the phone, which was no worse for two nights out in the cold weather, and hustled back to work. Along with my first cup of strong coffee I happily e-mailed my wife that we had found my phone. This would almost guarantee she would arrive at work later that morning in a very good mood; always a good thing for the person you sleep under the same sheets with!

Throughout the day I kept telling myself, *Leave that deer alone for at least a week.*

Do not go near the power line or your stand.

Don't bother checking the camera. You know his picture is on there, only a couple of hours ago you watched him scramble down the well-worn deer trail past the camera, past the food plot, and past your stand.

Just stay out of there and let him move back in.

I reluctantly took my own advice.

I waited.

It wasn't easy because bucks that size range pretty far during the rut and every neighbor I had would shoot that deer if given the chance. I couldn't blame them. He was at least a 130-inch class deer.

All the while I was waiting, I was thinking through my plan. I noted that the small group of plum bushes the buck was bedded in faces the southern sun. On a good cold day it was very likely the deer, after a busy night chasing does, would slip into that plum thicket right after dawn, enjoy good visual cover, a perfect escape route, and the warm morning sun.

I thought, *I need to beat him to that spot before good light and I need two phones!*

That's right, I would need to borrow my wife's phone. *Something*, I thought, *best done in the manner of asking for forgiveness instead of permission.*

On Thursday I stayed up to catch the eleven P.M. weather. Saturday coming, twenty-seven degrees for a low, warming to fifty-six by noon. The moon would be first quarter waxing. The sky would be clear. Perfect. It was a green light for Saturday!

Friday night while Claudia was taking a bath, I got her phone off the kitchen cabinet. I descended into the basement and practiced calling her phone. Her number was only a digit different from mine. This would make it easier to remember. I got it right on two consecutive tries, slipped it back in its place on the counter and laid out my hunting clothes for the next morning.

I figured false dawn would be about 6:20 A.M. I wanted to be sure I was in my stand by 6:00. I mentally calculated, an hour to shower, shave, dress, and drive, thirty minutes to get my wife's phone situated, ease into my ladder stand, load up, and let the woods quiet down. I set the alarm for 4:30 A.M.

Next morning I left my truck just inside the gate and hiked in. I was taking no chance of tipping this four-year-old off with a lot of tire crunching and engine noise. The moon's light reflecting off the hard frost turned the would-be darkness into a turquoise glimmer. The logo of a silver apple with one bite missing caught my eye as I set Claudia's freshly charged phone down as near to the plum thicket as I dared.

I hurried to my stand and hauled up my .270 Featherweight Winchester. As quietly as a mouse pissing on cotton I clicked two 160-grain rounds into the clip and one in the chamber, slipped the bolt forward and turned down the 3x10 Leupold scope to three power. Years earlier I had my scope mounted above the rifle's open sights. This morning, I felt it might prove to have been a wise move. The 16-foot-tall stand I was in was only fifty yards from the power line and the way that old boy tore out of those plum bushes last Monday I suspected he would be carrying the mail when he passed this way. The scope, even set on its lowest power, might not be an advantage. Unless the deer was standing still, I was predisposed to use the iron sights if he was moving fast.

The power line was off my left shoulder at ten o'clock. To my right at two o'clock stood a forty-year-old white oak. By 7:00 A.M. I had lost count of the gray squirrels cutting bright green acorns from its crown. Near eight o'clock a bachelor group of trophy gobblers with long beards began taking apart the four-inch-thick layer of white oak leaves beneath this tree creating a ruckus among the hardworking squirrels.

Unfortunately my stand was still in deep shade. I was just about to freeze to death when the most welcome sound of the morning reached my ears – two Carolina wrens began fussing over something or someone who was invading their space. I judged it to be right near the backdoor to the buck's plum bush hide. I gave the twin wrens twenty minutes to finally settle down. I figured if the buck was going to get in his usual bed he ought to be there by now.

I pulled my phone out of the left-hand pocket of my heavy hunting coat and dialed 704-1136. In the cold morning air I could hear my wife's phone ringing loud and clear. Showtime! I pushed off the safety of the .270, eased it up on the shooting rail of my stand with my left hand under the forearm, and put the stock deep into my right shoulder.

I was glad I was ready. That old buck came down the well-worn path as if his tail was on fire. I had to let him pass to get any kind of a side shot. I did not lead him enough on my first shot and saw the better part of a four-inch diameter pine disintegrate. I was a good foot behind the racing deer. I slid my right eye down to the open sights, lined them up on his massive right shoulder, pushed the muzzle way far ahead, and squeezed off the second round. The velocity of the bullet spun him completely around. He ran another thirty yards dead on his feet and piled up at the base of the white oak.

Still breathing hard and my pulse racing, I knelt beside the best deer of the season and ran my hand down his warm soft side. What a beautiful creature he was.

I just sat beside him for a while, admiring his near perfectly camouflaged brown- to-gray sides and pure white chin and neck. His antlers, a good 21 inches inside spread, had sharp polished ivory tips that faded to thick tan-and light-brown bases. He was at least four years old, a mature male in his prime and, no doubt, king of the hill in these parts.

Right then I realized my wife's phone was still ringing. On the spot I decided when bragging on this deer to never tell about the phone.

Nobody will believe it!

ACKNOWLEDGEMENTS

I need to recognize and thank the individuals that have made this book possible. Dorothy Smith has spent hours and hours transposing my unreadable handwriting into a legible manuscript. I am indebted to Clare Neely for her untiring effort as my editor, and Kirk Neely for his patient assistance. Also I am grateful to Kathy Green, for her suggestions that smoothed out many a rough spot.

I appreciate so much the time that Nancy Kochenower has spent in putting my ideas for each story into her beautiful sketches.

Dianne Kusztos, thank you for the wonderful work you have done on the cover design.

It is with a grateful heart that I want to recognize the contribution my friend Bob Timberlake has made to this book with his gracious foreword. Thank you, Bob.

Finally, my utmost thankfulness goes to my Lord, Jesus Christ, for all His goodness upon me and my family.

ABOUT THE AUTHOR

J ohn P. Faris, Jr. is a native of Laurens, South Carolina.

John received a Bachelor of Science degree from Georgia Tech and later earned his MBA.

While serving four years in the Navy, John married Claudia Tinsley, also of Laurens. Over the years they purchased several businesses and continue to work together at Oilmen's Equipment and Corrugated Containers.

John enjoys farming and boat building, however his passion since childhood has been hunting and fishing.

He and Claudia adore exploring new places. Over the past forty-seven years, in search of the next great adventure, they have visited all seven continents, over eighty countries, and circumnavigated the globe three times.

John lives with his family in Upstate South Carolina where he periodically updates his Web page at outdoorstories.com

NANCY KOCHENOWER
INTERNAL ILLUSTRATIONS

Nancy Kochenower is an award-winning artist who specializes in both oil and water-color portraits. Her work is found in museums, institutions, businesses, and private collections nationwide and has also been featured in local and national publications. She is a member of the Portrait Society of America and the Artists' Guild of Spartanburg.

Nancy's training began as a child when she developed an interest in drawing the human face and form. She began to paint using watercolors in 1972.

From 1988 until 1992 she taught private painting classes to both children and adults while working as a freelance illustrator.

In 1992 Nancy became a full-time portrait artist.

You can visit Nancy's Web site at www.nancykochenower.com

DIANNE KUSZTOS WILSON
COVER DESIGNER

Dianne Kusztos knew the first time she held a crayon that she was destined to be an artist. After graduating from the Ringling College of Art and Design in Sarasota, Florida, she secured a position as commercial artist with an ad agency in her hometown of Spartanburg, South Carolina, and soon became its art director.

One year later Dianne started Kusztos-Wilson Advertising and has spent the last twenty years changing with the times, utilizing her graphic design skills to promote well-respected companies such as Milliken & Company and Oilmen's Truck Tanks.

Dianne has been happily married for more than thirty years and is the proud mother of a daughter, who is also a graphic designer and partner in her business: KWDadvertising.com

TO ASHLEY AND JOHN

Thank you Ashley and John. From the time you were very young my love for you and the outdoors have been the motivation for countless adventures. Whether bream fishing in Poppa Tinsley's farm pond, or billfishing off Kona, Hawaii, from spending a day on a shrimp boat off Georgetown to camping in the backcountry along the Snake River, you have given Mom and me a gunnysack full of memories.

I pray that God will continue to give you and your children a love of His great outdoors and a passion for adventure.

Illustrations on this page
By
Ashley Faris Patterson

To those who come after, especially Ashley, John, Cameron, Kaleb, Joshua, Grace, and Bailey.

Twenty years from now you will be more disappointed by the things you didn't do than by the ones you did do. So throw off the bowlines, sail away from the safe harbor. Catch the trade winds in your sails.

Explore. Dream. Discover.

Mark Twain